COOKSHELF

Thai

Christine France

p

This is a Parragon Book
First published in 2001

Parragon
Queen Street House
4 Queen Street
Bath BA1 1HE, UK

Hardback ISBN: 0-75254-961-8
Paperback ISBN: 0-75254-981-2

Printed in China

NOTE

This book uses metric and imperial measurements.
Follow the same units of measurement throughout; do not mix metric and imperial.
All spoon measurements are level: teaspoons are assumed to be 5 ml, and tablespoons are assumed to be 15 ml.
Unless otherwise stated, milk is assumed to be full fat, eggs and individual vegetables
such as potatoes are medium, and pepper is freshly ground black pepper.

Recipes using raw or very lightly cooked eggs should be avoided by infants, the elderly,
pregnant women, convalescents, and anyone suffering from an illness.

Contents

Introduction

Anyone who has a love of Thai food will appreciate that it is a unique cuisine, distinctly different from the countries which border it geographically, but with many foreign influences. Many of its characteristics result from climate and culture, but centuries of invasions and emigration have played a large part in shaping Thai cuisine.

The roots of the Thai nation can be traced back to the first century, in the time of the Chinese Han Dynasty, when the T'ai tribes occupied parts of South China, along valuable trade routes between the East and West. Over the years, the T'ai had a close but often stormy relationship with the Chinese and, eventually, began to emigrate south to the lands of what is now northern Thailand, bordering Burma and Cambodia, then sparsely occupied by Buddhist and Hindu tribes.

Eventually, the T'ai established the independent Kingdom of Sukhothai (translated as 'dawn of happiness'), which eventually became known as Siam. The ports of Siam formed the entry to an important trade route, where ships from all over Europe and Japan docked in the coastal ports or sailed up the rivers bringing foreign foods, teas, spices, silks, copper and ceramics. It was the Portuguese who, in the sixteenth century, introduced the chilli to this part of the world, where the plants thrived and continues to thrive. Trade with Arab and Indian merchants was important, too, and many Muslims settled in Siam. The Kingdom of Siam survived until 1939, when it became the constitutional Thai monarchy.

Present-day Thailand still reflects much of these centuries of mixed cultures, and the Thai people are independent, proud, creative and passionate. Their love of life is clear in the way they take pleasure in entertaining and eating. They love to eat, at any time of day, and the streets are lined with food vendors selling a huge variety of tasty snacks from their stalls, carts or bicycles.

Thai people love parties and celebrations and during their many festivals, the colourful, often elaborate and carefully prepared festive foods show a respect for custom and tradition. Visitors are entertained with endless trays of tasty snacks, platters of exotic fruits and Thai beer or local whisky. When a meal is served, all the dishes are served up together, so the cook can enjoy the food along with the guests. Thais take pride in presenting food beautifully, often carving vegetables into elaborate shapes as garnishes. Their intricate and skilled artistry is an important part of Thai culture and shows a deep appreciation of beautiful things.

Everyday life in Thailand is closely tied to the seasons, marked by the harvesting of crops and vagaries of the monsoon climate. The Thai people take their food seriously, taking great care in choosing the freshest of ingredients and carefully balancing delicate flavours and textures. Throughout Thailand, rice is the most important staple food, the centre of every meal, and coconut, in its various forms, has an almost equal place. Cooks in every region are expert at making the very most of the food that's available locally, so the character of many classic Thai dishes will often vary, depending on the region.

FUNDAMENTALS OF THAI CUISINE

Essential ingredients when you're starting out to cook your own Thai cuisine are coconut, lime, chilli, rice, garlic, lemon grass, fresh root ginger and coriander, and with a basic supply of these you can create many typical Thai dishes. Although many recipes have quite long lists of ingredients, the methods of preparing and cooking are mostly simple enough for even an inexperienced cook to handle.

The main principle of Thai cooking is balance, the five extremes of flavour – bitter, sour, hot, salt and sweet – being carefully and skillfully balanced within a dish or over several courses, each dish contributing part of the whole perfect balance of the entire meal.

TYPICAL THAI FLAVOURINGS

BASIL

Three types of sweet basil are used in Thai cooking, but the sweet basil we can buy in the West also works well. Oriental food stores often sell the seeds for Thai basil, so you can grow your own.

CHILLIES

The many varieties of chilli vary in heat, from very mild to fiery hot, so choose carefully. The small red or green 'bird-eye' chillies often used in Thai dishes are very hot, so if you prefer a mild heat, remove the seeds. Red are generally slightly sweeter and milder than green. Larger chillies tend to be milder. Dried crushed chillies are used for seasoning.

COCONUT MILK

This is made from grated and pressed fresh coconut. It can be bought in cans and longlife packs, in powdered form or in blocks (creamed coconut). Coconut cream is skimmed from the top and is slightly thicker and richer.

CORIANDER

This is a fresh herb with a pungent, citrus-like flavour, widely used in savoury dishes. Try to buy it with a root attached.

GALANGAL

A relative of ginger with a milder, aromatic flavour. Available fresh or dried.

GARLIC

Garlic is used whole, crushed, sliced or chopped in savoury dishes and curry pastes. Pickled garlic is another useful item and makes an attractive garnish.

GINGER

Fresh root ginger is peeled and grated, chopped or sliced for a warm spicy flavour.

KAFFIR LIME LEAVES

The leaves have a distinctive lime scent, and can be bought fresh, dried or frozen.

LEMON GRASS

An aromatic tropical grass with a lemony scent similar to lemon balm. Strip off the fibrous outer leaves and slice or finely chop the rest, or bruise and use whole. It can also be bought in dried powdered form.

PALM SUGAR

This is a rich, brown unrefined sugar made from the coconut palm, sold in solid blocks, and the best way to use it is to crush it with a mallet or rolling pin. Muscovado sugar is a good substitute.

RICE VINEGAR

Also called 'mirin', this sweet rice vinegar is used as a savoury flavouring. Sherry or white wine vinegar can be used as a substitute.

SOY SAUCE

Both dark and light soy sauces are used for seasoning, but light is saltier than dark. Light soy sauce is used mainly in stir-fries or with light meats. Dark soy sauce adds a mature rich flavour and colour to braised and red meat dishes.

TAMARIND PASTE

The pulp of the tamarind fruit is usually sold in blocks. This gives a sour/sweet flavour. Soak the pulp in hot water for 30 minutes, press out the juice and discard the pulp and seeds.

THAI FISH SAUCE

Called *nam pla*, this is used like salt for seasoning and has a distinctive, intense aroma. It is made from salted fermented fish.

Snacks, Starters & Soups

The structure of a Thai meal is more flexible than in the West, with no starters and main courses as such; instead, soups, side dishes, noodles, rice and main dishes appear simultaneously. Small snacks or appetizers may be served as afternoon treats or offered to guests before they sit down for a meal.

Many of the recipes in this section are savoury snacks which are eaten at all times of day and at parties and celebrations. The Thais eat whenever they are hungry, and street vendors cater for this need with a huge and tempting array of wares from their stalls and bicycles – each street vendor has his own speciality of fast food, from crab cakes to spare ribs and from steamed mussels to rice soup.

Soups are part of almost every Thai meal, including breakfast. Lunch is frequently a bowl of soup, often a thin stock-based broth, usually spiked with red or green chillies, and with the addition of fine noodles, rice, egg strips or tiny fish balls, meat balls or cubes of tofu. In restaurants, soups are often served in a large 'firepot' with a central funnel of burning coals to keep the contents hot.

Tiger Prawn Rolls with Sweet Soy Sauce

Serves 4

INGREDIENTS

DIP
1 small fresh red bird-eye
  chilli, deseeded
1 tsp clear honey
4 tbsp soy sauce

ROLLS
2 tbsp fresh coriander leaves
1 garlic clove
1½ tsp Thai red curry paste
16 wonton wrappers

1 egg white, lightly beaten
16 raw peeled tiger prawns
  with tails
sunflower oil for deep-frying

1 To make the dip, finely chop the chilli, then mix with the honey and soy in a small bowl and stir well. Set aside until required.

2 To make the prawn rolls, finely chop the coriander and garlic and mix with the curry paste.

3 Brush each wonton wrapper with a little egg white and place a small dab of the coriander mixture in the centre. Place a tiger prawn on top.

4 Fold the wonton wrapper over, enclosing the prawn and leaving the tail exposed. Repeat with the other prawns.

5 Heat the oil to 180°C/ 350°F, or until a cube of bread turns golden in 30 seconds. Fry the prawns, in small batches, for about 1–2 minutes each until golden brown and crisp. Drain on kitchen paper and serve with the dip.

VARIATION

If you prefer, replace the wonton wrappers with filo pastry – use a long strip of pastry, place the paste and a prawn on one end, then brush with egg white and wrap the pastry around the prawn to enclose and then fry.

Prawn & Chicken Sesame Toasts

Makes 72 pieces

INGREDIENTS

4 boneless, skinless chicken thighs	2 tbsp chopped fresh coriander	12 slices white bread, crusts removed
100 g/3½ oz cooked peeled prawns	1 tbsp Thai fish sauce	8 tbsp sesame seeds
1 small egg, beaten	½ tsp ground black pepper	sunflower oil for frying
3 spring onions, finely chopped	¼ tsp salt	spring onion curls, shredded, to garnish
2 garlic cloves, crushed		

1 Place the chicken and prawns in a food processor and process until very finely chopped. Add the egg, spring onions, garlic, coriander, fish sauce, pepper and salt, and pulse for a few seconds to mix well. Transfer to a bowl.

2 Spread the chicken and prawn mixture evenly over the slices of bread, right to the edges. Scatter the sesame seeds over a plate and gently press the spread side of each slice of bread into them to coat evenly.

3 Using a sharp knife, cut the bread into small rectangles, making 6 per slice.

4 Heat a 1 cm/½ inch depth of oil in a wide frying pan until very hot. Fry the bread rectangles quickly, in batches, for 2–3 minutes until golden brown, turning them over once.

5 Drain the sesame toasts thoroughly on kitchen paper and serve hot, garnished with thinly shredded spring onion curls.

COOK'S TIP

If you're catering for a party, it's a good idea to make the toasts in advance, then store them in the refrigerator or freezer. Cover and refrigerate for up to 3 days, or place in a sealed container or polythene bag and freeze for up to 1 month. Thaw overnight in the refrigerator, then pop into a hot oven for about 5 minutes to reheat thoroughly.

Thai Fish Cakes with Hot Peanut Dip

Serves 4–5

INGREDIENTS

350 g/12 oz white fish fillet
   skinned, such as cod
   or haddock
1 tbsp Thai fish sauce
2 tsp Thai red curry paste
1 tbsp lime juice
1 garlic clove, crushed

4 dried kaffir lime
   leaves, crumbled
1 egg white
3 tbsp chopped fresh coriander
vegetable oil for shallow frying
salt and pepper
green salad leaves, to serve

PEANUT DIP
1 small fresh red chilli
1 tbsp light soy sauce
1 tbsp lime juice
1 tbsp soft light brown sugar
3 tbsp chunky peanut butter
4 tbsp coconut milk

1 Put the fish fillet in a food processor with the fish sauce, curry paste, lime juice, garlic, lime leaves and egg white, and process until a smooth paste forms.

2 Stir in the chopped fresh coriander and quickly process again until well mixed. Divide the mixture into 8–10 pieces and roll into balls, then flatten to make round patties and set aside.

3 To make the dip, halve and deseed the chilli, then chop finely. Place in a small pan with the remaining dip ingredients and heat gently, stirring constantly, until well blended. Adjust the seasoning to taste.

4 Heat the oil in a frying pan and fry the fish cakes, in batches, for 3–4 minutes on each side until golden brown. Drain on kitchen paper and serve them hot on a bed of green salad leaves with the chilli-flavoured peanut dip.

Steamed Crab Cakes

Serves 4

INGREDIENTS

1–2 banana leaves	2 tbsp fresh coriander, chopped	2 egg whites
2 garlic cloves, crushed	3 tbsp creamed coconut	1 egg yolk
1 tsp lemon grass, finely chopped	1 tbsp lime juice	8 fresh coriander leaves
½ tsp pepper	200 g/7 oz cooked crab meat, flaked	sunflower oil for deep-frying
	1 tbsp Thai fish sauce	chilli sauce dip, to serve

1 Use the banana leaves to line 8 x 100 ml/3½ fl oz ramekins or foil containers.

2 Mix together the garlic, lemon grass, pepper and coriander. Mash the creamed coconut with the lime juice until smooth. Stir it into the other ingredients with the crab meat and fish sauce.

3 In a clean, dry bowl, whisk the egg whites until stiff, then lightly and evenly fold them into the crab mixture.

4 Spoon the mixture into the ramekins or foil containers lined with banana leaves and press down lightly. Brush the tops with egg yolk and top each with a fresh coriander leaf.

5 Place in a steamer half-filled with boiling water, then cover with a lid and steam for 15 minutes or until firm to the touch. Pour off the excess liquid and remove the crab cakes from the ramekins or foil containers.

6 Heat the oil to 180°C/350°F or until a cube of bread browns in 30 seconds. Add the crab cakes and deep-fry for about 1 minute, turning them over once, until golden brown. Serve hot with a chilli sauce dip.

Thai-style
Open Crab Meat Sandwich

Serves 4

INGREDIENTS

2 tbsp lime juice

2 cm/¾ in piece fresh root
ginger, grated

2 cm/¾ inch piece lemon grass,
finely chopped

5 tbsp mayonnaise

2 large slices crusty bread

1 ripe avocado

150 g/5½ oz cooked
crab meat

pepper

fresh coriander sprigs, to garnish

1 Mix half the lime juice
with the ginger and
lemon grass. Add the
mayonnaise and mix well.

2 Spread 1 tablespoon of
mayonnaise smoothly
over each slice of bread.

3 Halve the avocado and
remove the stone. Peel
and slice the flesh thinly, then
arrange the slices on the
bread. Sprinkle the avocado
with lime juice.

4 Spoon the crab meat over
the avocado, then add
any remaining lime juice.
Spoon over the remaining
mayonnaise, season with
black pepper, top with a
coriander sprig to garnish
and serve immediately.

COOK'S TIP

*To make lime-and-
ginger-flavoured
mayonnaise, place 2 egg
yolks, 1 tablespoon lime
juice and ½ teaspoon grated
root ginger in a blender
goblet. With the motor
running, gradually add
300 ml/10 fl oz olive oil,
drop by drop, until the
mixture is thick and
smooth. Season with salt
and pepper.*

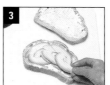

Mussels in Spiced Batter

Serves 4

INGREDIENTS

40 large live mussels
2 tbsp plain flour
2 tbsp rice flour
½ tsp salt
1 tbsp desiccated coconut

1 egg white
1 tbsp rice wine
2 tbsp water
1 small fresh red bird-eye chilli,
    deseeded and chopped

1 tbsp fresh coriander, chopped
sunflower oil for deep-frying
lime wedges, to serve

1 Thoroughly clean the mussels and discard any that do not close when tapped or appear to be damaged. Rinse in cold water and place in a pan, cover and steam over a high heat for 2–3 minutes, shaking the pan occasionally, until the mussels open. Drain, then remove from the shells. Discard any that are not open.

2 For the batter, strain together the plain flour, rice flour and salt into a bowl. Add the coconut, egg white, rice wine and water, and beat the ingredients until well mixed and a batter forms. Stir the chilli and coriander into the batter.

3 Heat a 5 cm/2 in depth of oil in a large pan to 180°C/350°F or until a cube of bread browns in 30 seconds. Holding the mussels with a fork, dip them quickly into the batter, then drop into the hot oil and fry for 1–2 minutes until crisp and golden brown.

4 Drain the mussels on kitchen paper and serve hot with lime wedges to squeeze over.

COOK'S TIP

If you reserve the mussel shells, the cooked mussels can be replaced in them to serve.

Steamed Mussels with Lemon Grass & Basil

Serves 4

INGREDIENTS

1 kg/2 lb 4 oz live mussels
2 shallots, finely chopped
1 lemon grass stalk, thinly sliced
1 garlic clove, finely chopped
3 tbsp rice wine or sherry

2 tbsp lime juice
1 tbsp Thai fish sauce
2 tbsp butter
4 tbsp chopped fresh basil
salt and pepper

fresh basil leaves, to garnish
crusty bread, to serve

1 Clean the mussels, removing any beards and dirt. Rinse in clear water and drain. Discard any that do not close when tapped, or have damaged shells.

2 Place the shallots, lemon grass, garlic, rice wine, lime juice and fish sauce in a large pan and place over a high heat.

3 Add the mussels, cover with a lid and steam the mussels for about 2–3 minutes, shaking the pan occasionally during cooking until the mussel shells open.

4 Discard any mussels which have not opened, then stir in the chopped basil and season with salt and pepper.

5 Scoop out the mussels with a perforated spoon and divide between 4 deep bowls. Quickly whisk the butter into the pan juices, then pour the juices over the mussels.

6 Garnish each bowl with fresh basil leaves and serve with plenty of crusty bread to mop up the juices.

COOK'S TIP

If you prefer to serve this dish as a main course, this amount will be enough for two portions. Fresh clams in shells are also very good when cooked by this method.

Roasted Spare Ribs with Honey & Soy

Serves 4

INGREDIENTS

1 kg/2 lb 4 oz Chinese-style spare ribs	2 garlic cloves, peeled	1 tbsp sesame oil
½ lemon	1 small onion, chopped	lemon twists, to garnish
½ small orange	2 tbsp soy sauce	orange wedges, to serve
2.5 cm/1 in piece fresh root ginger, peeled	2 tbsp rice wine	
	½ tsp Thai seven-spice powder	
	2 tbsp clear honey	

1 Place the ribs in a wide roasting tin, cover loosely with foil and cook in a preheated oven, 180°C/350°F/Gas Mark 4, for 30 minutes.

2 Meanwhile, remove any pips from the lemon and orange, and place the fruits in a food processor, together with the ginger, garlic, onion, soy sauce, rice wine, seven-spice powder, honey and sesame oil. Process until smooth.

3 Pour off any fat from the spare ribs, then spoon the puréed mixture over the spare ribs.

4 Toss the ribs to coat evenly. Return the ribs to the oven, increase the temperature to 200°C/400°F/Gas Mark 6 and roast, turning and basting them occasionally, for about 40 minutes or until golden brown. Garnish with lemon twists and serve hot with orange wedges.

COOK'S TIP

If you don't have a food processor, grate the rind and squeeze the juice from the citrus fruits, grate the ginger, crush the garlic and finely chop the onion. Mix these ingredients together with the remaining ingredients.

Steamed Wonton Bundles

Serves 4

INGREDIENTS

125 g/4½ oz minced pork
1 tbsp dried prawns,
    finely chopped
1 fresh green chilli,
    finely chopped

2 shallots, finely chopped
1 tsp cornflour
1 small egg, beaten
2 tsp dark soy sauce
2 tsp rice wine

12 wonton wrappers
1 tsp sesame oil
salt and pepper
spicy dip, to serve

1 Mix together the pork, dried shrimp, chilli and shallots. Blend the cornflour with half the egg and stir into the pork mixture, together with the soy sauce and rice wine. Season to taste with salt and pepper.

2 Arrange the wonton wrappers flat on a work surface and place about 1 tablespoon of the pork mixture on to the centre of each wrapper.

3 Brush the wrappers with the remaining egg and pull up the edges, pinching together lightly at the top and leaving a small gap so the filling can just be seen.

4 Pour water into the bottom of a steamer and bring to the boil. Brush the inside of the top part with sesame oil.

5 Arrange the wontons in the top, cover and steam for 15–20 minutes. Serve hot, with a spicy dip.

COOK'S TIP

Make sure that the water in the base of the steamer is not allowed to go off the boil, or the dumplings will be undercooked and soggy. Also keep an eye on it so that it doesn't boil dry – top up with extra boiling water if necessary.

Crispy Pork & Peanut Baskets

Serves 4

INGREDIENTS

2 sheets filo pastry, each about
    42 x 28 cm/16½ x 11 inches
2 tbsp vegetable oil
1 garlic clove, crushed
125 g/4½ oz minced pork
1 tsp Thai red curry paste

2 spring onions, finely chopped
3 tbsp crunchy peanut butter
1 tbsp light soy sauce

1 tbsp chopped fresh coriander
salt and pepper
fresh coriander sprigs, to garnish

1 Cut each sheet of filo pastry into 24 x 7 cm/2¾ inch squares, to make a total of 48 squares. Brush each square lightly with oil, and arrange the squares in stacks of 4 in 12 small patty tins, pointing outwards. Press the pastry down into the patty tins.

2 Bake the pastry cases in a preheated oven, 200°C/400°F/Gas Mark 6, for about 6–8 minutes until they are golden brown.

3 Meanwhile, heat 1 tablespoon oil in a wok. Add the garlic and fry for 30 seconds, then stir in the pork and stir-fry over a high heat for 4–5 minutes until the all the meat is golden brown.

4 Add the curry paste and spring onions and continue to stir-fry for a further 1 minute, then stir in the peanut butter, soy sauce and coriander. Season to taste with salt and pepper.

5 Spoon the pork mixture into the filo baskets and serve hot, garnished with coriander sprigs.

COOK'S TIP

Filo pastry dries out very quickly and becomes brittle and difficult to handle. Work quickly and keep any sheets of pastry you're not using covered with clingfilm and a dampened cloth.

Sticky Ginger Chicken Wings

Serves 4

INGREDIENTS

2 garlic cloves, peeled
1 piece stem ginger in
    syrup, drained
1 tsp coriander seeds
2 tbsp stem ginger syrup

2 tbsp dark soy sauce
1 tbsp lime juice
1 tsp sesame oil
12 chicken wings

TO GARNISH
lime wedges
fresh coriander leaves

1 Roughly chop the garlic and ginger. In a pestle and mortar, crush the garlic, stem ginger and coriander seeds to a paste, gradually working in the ginger syrup, soy sauce, lime juice and sesame oil.

2 Tuck the pointed tip of each chicken wing underneath the thicker end of the wing to make a neat triangular shape. Place in a large bowl.

3 Add the garlic and ginger paste to the bowl and toss the chicken wings in the mixture to coat evenly. Cover and leave in the refrigerator to marinate for several hours or overnight.

4 Arrange the chicken wings in a single layer on a foil-lined grill pan and grill under a preheated medium-hot grill, turning the wings occasionally, for about 12–15 minutes until they are golden brown and thoroughly cooked.

5 Alternatively, cook on a lightly oiled barbecue grill over medium-hot coals for 12–15 minutes. To serve, garnish with lime wedges and fresh coriander.

COOK'S TIP

To test if the chicken is cooked, pierce it deeply through the thickest part of the flesh. When fully cooked, the chicken juices are clear, with no trace of pink. If there is any trace of pink, cook for a few more minutes.

Stuffed Chicken Wings

Serves 4

INGREDIENTS

8 chicken wings	½ tsp salt	sunflower oil for deep-frying
3 tbsp dried prawns	½ tsp pepper	fresh red chillies, to garnish
3 tbsp hot water	2 spring onions, finely chopped	
200 g/7 oz minced pork	¼ tsp turmeric	TO SERVE
1 garlic clove, crushed	1 small egg, beaten	sweet chilli dipping sauce
1 tbsp Thai fish sauce	2 tbsp rice flour	cucumber slices

1 Using a small sharp knife, cut around the end of the bone at the cut end of each wing, then loosen the flesh from around the bone, scraping it downwards with the knife and pulling back the skin as you go. When you reach the next joint, grasp the end of the bone and twist sharply to break it at the joint. Remove the bone and turn back the flesh.

2 Continue to scrape the meat away down the length of the next long bone, exposing the joint. Twist to break the bone at the joint and remove, leaving just the wing tip in place.

3 Meanwhile, soak the dried prawns in the hot water for 10–15 minutes. Drain, then chop. Place the pork, prawns, garlic, fish sauce, salt and pepper into a food processor and process to a smooth paste. Scrape the mixture into a bowl and add the spring onions. Stir thoroughly to mix.

4 Stuff the chicken wings with the mixture, pressing it well down inside with your finger.

5 Beat the turmeric into the egg. Dip each wing into the rice flour, shaking off the excess.

6 Heat a 5 cm/2 inch depth of oil in a large pan to 190°C/375°F or until a cube of bread browns in 30 seconds. Dip the floured chicken wings quickly into the turmeric-flavoured egg, then drop carefully into the hot oil and fry, in small batches, for about 8–10 minutes, turning them over once.

7 Drain the chicken wings on kitchen paper. Garnish with fresh red chillies and serve hot or cold with sliced cucumber and a sweet chilli dipping sauce.

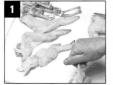

Lemon Grass Chicken Skewers

Serves 4

INGREDIENTS

2 long or 4 short lemon grass stalks	1 carrot, finely grated	1 tbsp sunflower oil
2 large boneless, skinless chicken breasts, about 400 g/14 oz in total	1 small fresh red chilli, deseeded and chopped	salt and pepper
1 small egg white	2 tbsp chopped fresh garlic chives	TO GARNISH
	2 tbsp chopped fresh coriander	fresh coriander sprigs
		lime slices

1 If the lemon grass stalks are long, cut them in half across the middle to make 4 short lengths. Cut each stalk in half lengthways, so you have 8 sticks.

2 Roughly chop the chicken pieces and place them in a food processor with the egg white. Process to a smooth paste, then add the carrot, chilli, chives and coriander and season with salt and pepper to taste. Process for a few seconds to mix well.

3 Chill the mixture in the refrigerator for about 15 minutes. Divide the mixture into 8 equal portions, and use your hands to shape the mixture around the lemon grass 'skewers'.

4 Brush the skewers with oil and grill under a preheated medium-hot grill, turning them occasionally, for 4–6 minutes until golden brown and thoroughly cooked. Alternatively, barbecue the skewers over medium-hot coals.

5 Serve immediately, garnished with coriander sprigs and slices of lime.

COOK'S TIP

If you can't find whole lemon grass stalks, use wooden or bamboo skewers instead, and add ½ teaspoon ground lemon grass to the mixture with the other flavourings.

Chicken Roasted in Banana Leaves

Serves 4–6

INGREDIENTS

1 garlic clove, chopped
1 tsp finely chopped fresh
    root ginger
¼ tsp pepper
2 fresh coriander sprigs

1 tbsp Thai fish sauce
1 tbsp whisky
3 boneless, skinless
    chicken breasts

2–3 banana leaves, cut into
    7.5 cm/3 in squares
sunflower oil, for frying
sweet chilli dipping sauce,
    to serve

1 Place the garlic, ginger, pepper, coriander sprigs, fish sauce and whisky in a mortar and grind the ingredients to a smooth paste with a pestle.

2 Cut the chicken into 2.5 cm/1 inch chunks and toss in the paste to coat evenly. Cover and place in the refrigerator to marinate for about 1 hour.

3 Place a piece of chicken on a square of banana leaf and wrap it up like a parcel to enclose the chicken completely. Secure with wooden cocktail sticks or tie the parcel with a piece of bamboo string.

4 Heat a 3 mm/⅛ inch depth of oil in a heavy-based frying pan until hot.

5 Fry the parcels, turning them over occasionally, for about 8–10 minutes until golden brown and the chicken is thoroughly cooked. Serve with a sweet chilli dipping sauce.

COOK'S TIP

To make a sweet chilli dip to serve with the chicken pieces, mix together equal amounts of chilli sauce and tomato ketchup, then stir in a dash of rice wine to taste.

Chicken Balls with Dipping Sauce

Serves 4–6

INGREDIENTS

2 large boneless, skinless
   chicken breasts
3 tbsp vegetable oil
2 shallots, finely chopped
½ celery stick, finely chopped
1 garlic clove, crushed

2 tbsp light soy sauce
1 small egg
1 bunch spring onions
salt and pepper
spring onion tassels,
   to garnish

DIPPING SAUCE
3 tbsp dark soy sauce
1 tbsp rice wine
1 tsp sesame seeds

1 Cut the chicken into 2 cm/¾ inch pieces. Heat half of the oil in a frying pan or wok and stir-fry the chicken over a high heat for 2–3 minutes until golden. Remove from the pan or wok with a perforated spoon and set aside.

2 Add the shallots, celery and garlic to the pan and stir-fry for 1–2 minutes until softened but not browned.

3 Place the chicken, shallots, celery and garlic in a food processor and process until finely minced. Add 1 tablespoon of the light soy sauce, just enough egg to make a fairly firm mixture, and salt and pepper to taste.

4 Trim the spring onions and cut into 5 cm/2 inch lengths. Make the dipping sauce by mixing together the dark soy sauce, rice wine and sesame seeds and set aside.

5 With your hands, shape the chicken mixture into 16–18 walnut-size balls. Heat the remaining oil in the frying pan or wok and stir-fry the balls, in small batches, for 4–5 minutes until golden brown. As each batch is cooked drain on kitchen paper and keep hot.

6 Stir-fry the spring onions for 1–2 minutes until they begin to soften, then stir in the remaining light soy sauce. Serve with the chicken balls and dipping sauce on a platter, garnished with the spring onion tassels.

Stuffed Eggs with Pork & Crab Meat

Serves 4

INGREDIENTS

4 large eggs
100 g/3½ oz minced pork
175 g/6 oz can white crab
   meat, drained
1 garlic clove, crushed
1 tsp Thai fish sauce
½ tsp ground lemon grass

1 tbsp chopped fresh coriander
1 tbsp desiccated coconut
100 g/3½ oz plain flour
about 150 ml/5 fl oz coconut
   milk
salt and pepper
sunflower oil, for deep-frying

cucumber flower, to garnish
green salad, to serve

1 Place the eggs in a small pan of simmering water and bring to the boil, then simmer for 10 minutes. Drain the eggs, crack the shells slightly and cool under cold running water. Peel off the shells.

2 Cut the eggs lengthways down the middle and scoop out the yolks. Place the yolks in a bowl with the pork, crab meat, garlic, fish sauce, lemon grass, coriander and coconut. Season with salt and pepper to taste and mix the ingredients together well.

3 Divide the mixture into 8 equal portions, then fill each of the egg whites with the mixture, pressing together with your hands to form the shape of a whole egg.

4 Whisk together the flour and enough coconut milk to make a thick coating batter, seasoning with salt and pepper. Heat a 5 cm/ 2 inch depth of oil in a large pan to 190°C/375°F or until a cube of bread browns in 30 seconds. Dip each egg into the coconut batter, then shake off the excess.

5 Fry the eggs, in batches, turning occasionally, for about 5 minutes until golden brown. Remove with a perforated spoon and drain on kitchen paper. Serve the eggs either warm or cold, garnished with cucumber flowers and accompanied by a green salad.

Thai-stuffed Omelette

Serves 4

INGREDIENTS

2 garlic cloves, chopped

4 black peppercorns

4 fresh coriander sprigs

2 tbsp vegetable oil

200 g/7 oz minced pork

2 spring onions, chopped

1 large, firm tomato, chopped

6 large eggs

1 tbsp Thai fish sauce

¼ tsp turmeric

mixed salad leaves, tossed,
   to serve

1 Place the garlic, peppercorns and coriander in a mortar and crush with a pestle until a smooth paste forms.

2 Heat 1 tablespoon of the oil in a wok over a medium heat. Add the paste and fry for 1–2 minutes until it just changes colour.

3 Stir in the minced pork and stir-fry until it is lightly browned. Add the spring onions and tomato and stir-fry for a further minute, then remove from the heat and set aside.

4 Heat the remaining oil in a small, heavy-based frying pan. Beat the eggs with the fish sauce and turmeric, then pour a quarter of the egg mixture into the pan. As the mixture begins to set, stir lightly to ensure that all the liquid egg is set.

5 Spoon a quarter of the pork mixture down the centre of the omelette, then fold the sides inwards towards the centre, enclosing the filling. Make 3 more omelettes with the remaining eggs and fill with the remaining pork mixture.

6 Slide the omelettes on to serving plates and serve with mixed salad leaves.

COOK'S TIP

If you prefer, spread half the pork mixture evenly over one omelette, then place a second omelette on top, without folding. Cut into slim wedges to serve.

Vegetarian Spring Rolls

Serves 4

INGREDIENTS

25 g/1 oz fine cellophane noodles	1 small carrot, finely shredded	½ tsp cornflour
2 tbsp groundnut oil	½ tsp sesame oil	groundnut oil, for deep-frying
2 garlic cloves, crushed	1 tbsp light soy sauce	fresh mint sprigs, to garnish
½ tsp grated fresh root ginger	1 tbsp rice wine or dry sherry	
55 g/2 oz oyster mushrooms, thinly sliced	¼ tsp pepper	
2 spring onions, finely chopped	1 tbsp chopped fresh coriander	
50g/1¾ oz beansprouts	1 tbsp chopped fresh mint	
	24 spring-roll wrappers	

1 Place the noodles in a heatproof bowl, pour over enough boiling water to cover and leave to stand for 4 minutes. Drain, rinse in cold water, then drain again. Cut or snip the noodles into 5 cm/2 inch lengths.

2 Heat the groundnut oil in a wok or wide pan over a high heat. Add the garlic, ginger, oyster mushrooms, spring onions, beansprouts and carrot and stir-fry for about 1 minute until just softened.

3 Stir in the sesame oil, soy sauce, rice wine, pepper, chopped coriander and mint, then remove the pan from the heat. Stir in the rice noodles.

4 Arrange the spring-roll wrappers on a work surface, pointing diagonally. Mix the cornflour with 1 tablespoon water to a smooth paste and brush the edges of 1 wrapper with it. Spoon a little filling on to the pointed side of the same wrapper.

5 Roll the point of the wrapper over the filling, then fold the side points inwards over the filling. Continue to roll up the wrapper away from you, moistening the tip with a little more cornflour paste to secure the roll.

6 Heat the oil in a wok or deep frying pan to 180°C/350°F or until a cube of bread browns in 30 seconds. Add the rolls, in batches, and deep-fry for 2–3 minutes each until golden and crisp.

Sweet-and-Sour Seafood Salad

Serves 6

INGREDIENTS

18 live mussels	¼ cucumber	2 tbsp Thai fish sauce
6 large scallops	1 carrot	1 tsp sesame oil
200 g/7 oz baby squid, cleaned	¼ head Chinese leaves, shredded	1 tbsp soft light brown sugar
2 shallots, finely chopped		2 tbsp chopped fresh mint
6 raw tiger prawns, peeled	DRESSING	¼ tsp pepper
and de-veined	4 tbsp lime juice	salt
	2 garlic cloves, finely chopped	

1 Clean the mussels, discarding any damaged or open ones that do not close when firmly tapped. Steam them in just the water which clings to them for 1–2 minutes until opened. Lift out with a perforated spoon, reserving the liquid in the pan. Discard any mussels that have not opened.

2 Separate the corals from the scallops and cut the whites in half horizontally. Cut the tentacles from the squid and slice the body cavities into rings.

3 Add the shallots to the liquid in the pan and simmer over a high heat until the liquid is reduced to about 3 tablespoons. Add the scallops, squid and tiger prawns and stir for about 2–3 minutes until cooked. Remove and spoon the mixture into a wide bowl.

4 Cut the cucumber and carrot in half lengthways, then slice thinly on a diagonal angle to make long, pointed slices. Toss with the Chinese leaves.

5 To make the dressing, place all the ingredients in a screw-top jar and shake well until evenly combined. Season with salt.

6 Toss the vegetables and seafood together. Spoon the dressing over the vegetables and seafood and serve immediately.

Warm Salad of Tuna & Tomatoes with Ginger Dressing

Serves 4

INGREDIENTS

50 g/1¾ oz Chinese
    leaves, shredded
3 tbsp rice wine
2 tbsp Thai fish sauce
1 tbsp fresh root ginger,
    finely shredded

1 garlic clove, finely chopped
½ small fresh red bird-eye chilli,
    finely chopped
2 tsp soft light brown sugar
2 tbsp lime juice
400 g/14 oz fresh tuna steak

sunflower oil, for brushing
125 g/4½ oz cherry tomatoes

TO GARNISH
fresh mint leaves
roughly chopped fresh mint

1 Place a small pile of shredded Chinese leaves on a serving plate. Place the rice wine, fish sauce, ginger, garlic, chilli, sugar and 1 tablespoon of the lime juice in a screw-top jar and shake vigorously to combine evenly.

2 Cut the tuna into strips of an even thickness. Sprinkle with the remaining lime juice.

3 Brush a wide frying pan or griddle with oil and heat until very hot. Add the tuna strips to the pan or griddle and cook until just firm and light golden, turning them over once. Remove and set aside.

4 Add the tomatoes to the pan or griddle and cook over a high heat until lightly browned. Spoon the tuna and tomatoes over the Chinese leaves and spoon over the dressing. Garnish with fresh mint and serve warm.

COOK'S TIP

You can make a quick version of this dish using canned tuna. Just drain and flake the tuna, omit steps 2 and 3 and continue as in the recipe.

Chilli-spiced Prawn Wonton Soup

Serves 4

INGREDIENTS

WONTONS
175 g/6 oz peeled cooked prawns
1 garlic clove, crushed
1 spring onion,
    finely chopped
1 tbsp dark soy sauce
1 tbsp Thai fish sauce
1 tbsp chopped fresh coriander

1 small egg, separated
12 wonton wrappers

SOUP
2 small fresh red bird-eye chillies
2 spring onions
1 litre/1¾ pints clear beef stock
1 tbsp Thai fish sauce

1 tbsp dark soy sauce
1 tbsp rice wine
fresh coriander leaves, to garnish

1 Finely chop the prawns. Put them in a small bowl and add the garlic, spring onion, soy sauce, fish sauce, chopped coriander and egg yolk. Stir well to mix.

2 Lay the wonton wrappers on a work surface in a single layer and place about 1 tablespoon of the filling mixture in the middle of each. Brush the edges with egg white and fold each into a triangle, pressing lightly to seal. Bring the 2 bottom corners of the triangle around to meet in the middle, securing with a little more egg white to hold in place.

3 For the soup, slice the chillies at a steep diagonal angle to make long thin slices, removing the seeds if you prefer a milder flavour. Slice the spring onions on the same steep diagonal angle.

4 Place the stock, fish sauce, soy sauce and rice wine in a large pan and bring to the boil over a medium heat. Add the chillies and spring onions. Drop the wontons into the pan and simmer for 4–5 minutes until thoroughly heated.

5 Ladle the soup and wontons in small bowls. Scatter fresh coriander leaves over the bowls and serve immediately.

Hot & Sour Soup

Serves 4

INGREDIENTS

350 g/12 oz whole raw or cooked
    prawns in shells
1 tbsp vegetable oil
1 lemon grass stalk,
    roughly chopped
2 kaffir lime leaves, shredded

1 fresh green chilli, deseeded and
    chopped
1.2 litres/2 pints chicken or
    fish stock
1 lime
1 tbsp Thai fish sauce

1 fresh red bird-eye chilli,
    deseeded and thinly sliced
1 spring onion, thinly sliced
salt and pepper
1 tbsp finely chopped coriander,
    to garnish

1 Peel the prawns and remove the heads. Reserve the shells. De-vein the prawns, cover and chill.

2 Heat the oil in a large pan and stir-fry the prawn shells for 3–4 minutes until they turn pink. Add the lemon grass, lime leaves, chilli and stock. Pare a thin strip of rind from the lime and grate the rest. Add the grated rind to the pan.

3 Bring to the boil, then lower the heat, cover and simmer gently for about 20 minutes.

4 Strain the liquid and pour it back into the pan. Squeeze the juice from the lime and add to the pan with the fish sauce. Season with salt and pepper to taste.

5 Bring the mixture in the pan to the boil. Lower the heat, add the prawns and simmer for 2–3 minutes.

6 Add the thinly sliced chilli and spring onion.

Ladle the soup into small bowls, sprinkle with the chopped coriander and serve.

COOK'S TIP

To de-vein the prawns, remove the shells. Cut a slit along the back of each prawn and remove the fine black vein that runs along the length of the back. Wipe with kitchen paper.

Creamy Sweetcorn Soup with Egg

Serves 4

INGREDIENTS

1 tbsp vegetable oil
3 garlic cloves, crushed
1 tsp grated fresh root ginger
700 ml/1¼ pints chicken stock
375 g/13 oz can
    creamed sweetcorn

1 tbsp Thai fish sauce
170 g/6 oz can white crab
    meat, drained
1 egg
salt and pepper

TO GARNISH
shredded fresh coriander
paprika

1 Heat the oil in a large saucepan and fry the garlic for 1 minute, stirring constantly.

2 Add the ginger to the pan, then stir in the stock and creamed sweetcorn. Bring to the boil.

3 Stir in the fish sauce, crab meat and salt and pepper, then return the soup to the boil.

4 Beat the egg, then stir lightly into the soup so it sets into long strands. Simmer gently for about 30 seconds until just set.

5 Ladle the soup into bowls and serve hot, garnished with shredded coriander and paprika sprinkled over.

COOK'S TIP

To give the soup an extra rich flavour for a special occasion, stir in 1 tablespoon of dry sherry or rice wine just before you ladle it into bowls.

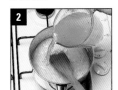

Pumpkin & Coconut Soup

Serves 6

INGREDIENTS

1 kg/2 lb 4 oz pumpkin	1 large onion, chopped	1 tbsp dried shrimp
1 tbsp groundnut oil	1 celery stick, chopped	5 tbsp coconut cream
1 tsp yellow mustard seeds	1 small red chilli, chopped	salt and pepper
1 garlic clove, crushed	850 ml/1½ pints stock	extra coconut cream, to garnish

1 Halve the pumpkin and remove the seeds. Cut away the skin and dice the flesh.

2 Heat the oil in a large flameproof casserole and fry the mustard seeds until they begin to pop. Stir in the garlic, onion, celery and chilli, and stir-fry for 1–2 minutes.

3 Add the pumpkin with the stock and dried prawns and bring to the boil. Lower the heat, cover and simmer gently for about 30 minutes until all the ingredients are very tender.

4 Transfer the mixture to a food processor or blender and process until smooth. Return the mixture to the pan and stir in the coconut cream.

5 Adjust the seasoning to taste with salt and pepper and serve hot, with coconut cream swirled in each bowl.

COOK'S TIP

For an extra touch of garnish, swirl a spoonful of thick coconut milk into each bowl of soup as you serve it.

Mushroom & Tofu Broth

Serves 4

INGREDIENTS

4 dried black mushrooms
1 tbsp sunflower oil
1 tsp sesame oil
1 garlic clove, crushed
1 fresh green chilli, deseeded and
    finely chopped
6 spring onions

1 litre/1¾ pints rich brown stock
85 g/3 oz fresh oyster
    mushrooms, sliced
2 kaffir lime leaves,
    finely shredded
2 tbsp lime juice
1 tbsp rice vinegar

1 tbsp Thai fish sauce
85 g/3 oz firm tofu, diced
salt and pepper

1 Pour 150 ml/5 fl oz boiling water over the dried black mushrooms in a heatproof bowl and leave to soak for about 30 minutes. Drain, reserving the liquid, then chop the black mushrooms roughly.

2 Heat the sunflower and sesame oils in a large pan or wok over a high heat. Add the garlic, chilli and spring onions and stir-fry for about 1 minute until softened, but not browned.

3 Add all of the mushrooms, kaffir lime leaves, stock and reserved mushroom liquid. Bring to the boil.

4 Stir in the lime juice, rice vinegar and fish sauce, lower the heat and simmer gently for 3–4 minutes.

5 Add the diced tofu and adjust the seasoning to taste with salt and pepper. Heat gently until boiling, then serve immediately.

COOK'S TIP

Use a clear, richly coloured home-made beef stock, or alternatively a Japanese dashi, to make an attractive clear broth. Stock cubes generally make a cloudy stock. To make a vegetarian version of the broth, use a well-flavoured vegetable stock and replace the fish sauce with light soy sauce.

Rice Soup with Eggs

Serves 4

INGREDIENTS

1 tsp sunflower oil
1 garlic clove, crushed
50 g/1¾ oz minced pork
3 spring onions, sliced
1 tbsp grated fresh root ginger
1 fresh red bird-eye chilli,
    deseeded and chopped

1 litre/1¾ pints chicken stock
200 g/7 oz cooked long-grain rice
1 tbsp Thai fish sauce
4 small eggs

salt and pepper
2 tbsp shredded fresh coriander,
    to garnish

1 Heat the oil in a large pan or wok. Add the garlic and stir-fry over a low heat for about 1 minute until the meat is broken up, but not browned.

2 Stir in the spring onions, ginger, chilli and stock and bring to the boil, stirring constantly. Add the rice, lower the heat and simmer for 2 minutes.

3 Add the fish sauce and adjust the seasoning with salt and pepper to taste. Carefully break the eggs into the soup and simmer over a very low heat for about 3–4 minutes until set.

4 Ladle the soup into large bowls, allowing 1 egg per portion. Sprinkle with the shredded coriander to garnish and serve.

COOK'S TIP

If you prefer, beat the eggs together and fry like an omelette until set, then cut into ribbon-like strips and add to the soup just before serving.

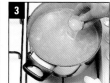

Spinach & Ginger Soup

Serves 4

INGREDIENTS

2 tbsp sunflower oil
1 onion, chopped
2 garlic cloves, finely chopped
2.5 cm/1 in piece fresh root
　ginger, finely chopped
250 g/9 oz fresh young
　spinach leaves

1 small lemon grass stalk,
　finely chopped
1 litre/1¾ pints chicken or
　vegetable stock
1 small potato, peeled
　and chopped

1 tbsp rice wine or dry sherry
1 tsp sesame oil
salt and pepper
finely shredded fresh spinach,
　to garnish

1 Heat the oil in a large saucepan. Add the onion, garlic and ginger, and fry gently for 3–4 minutes until softened, but not browned.

2 Reserve 2–3 small spinach leaves. Add the remaining leaves and lemon grass to the saucepan, stirring until the spinach is wilted. Add the stock and potato to the pan and bring to the boil. Lower the heat, cover and simmer for about 10 minutes.

3 Tip the soup into a blender or food processor and process until completely smooth.

4 Return the soup to the pan and add the rice wine, then adjust the seasoning to taste with salt and pepper. Heat until just below boiling point.

5 Finely shred the reserved spinach leaves and scatter some over the top. Drizzle with a few drops of sesame oil and serve hot, garnished with the finely shredded fresh spinach leaves.

VARIATION

To make a creamy-textured spinach and coconut soup, stir in about 4 tablespoons creamed coconut, or alternatively replace about 300 ml/ 10 fl oz of the stock with coconut milk. Serve the soup with shavings of fresh coconut scattered over the surface.

Chilled Avocado, Lime & Coriander Soup

Serves 4

INGREDIENTS

2 ripe avocados
1 small mild onion, chopped
1 garlic clove, crushed
2 tbsp chopped fresh coriander
1 tbsp chopped fresh mint
2 tbsp lime juice

700 ml/1¼ pints vegetable stock
1 tbsp rice vinegar
1 tbsp light soy sauce
salt and pepper

TO GARNISH

2 tbsp soured cream or
    crème fraîche
1 tbsp finely chopped
    fresh coriander
2 tsp lime juice
lime rind, finely shredded

1 Halve, stone and scoop out the flesh from the avocados. Place in a blender or food processor with the onion, garlic, coriander, mint, lime juice and about half the stock and process until completely smooth.

2 Add the remaining stock, rice vinegar and soy sauce and process again to mix well. Taste and adjust the seasoning, if necessary,

with salt and pepper or with a little extra lime juice if required. Cover and chill in the refrigerator until needed.

3 To make the lime and coriander cream garnish, mix together the soured cream or crème fraîche, coriander and lime juice. Spoon into the soup just before serving and sprinkle with lime rind.

COOK'S TIP

The top surface of the soup may darken slightly if the soup is stored for longer than about an hour, but don't worry – just give it a quick stir before serving. If you plan to keep the soup for several hours, lay a piece of clingfilm over the surface to seal it from the air.

Meat Fish & Main Dishes

The Thais are primarily a fish-eating nation and meat takes a back seat in most meals, except for special celebrations. The waterways of Thailand are teeming with many types of fish – even in the channels between the rice paddy fields – and the warm seas bring an abundance of fish and shellfish. So it's hardly surprising that along with rice, fish has long been a vital part of the Thai diet.

Even in the heart of Bangkok city, the markets are packed with fresh fish and seafood of all kinds. In Thai coastal towns, rows of thatch-roofed beach kiosks sell every type of fresh seafood from the warm Gulf waters, from barbecued or sautéed fish with ginger, prawns in coconut milk and coriander to steamed crab, to locals and visitors alike.

Because of the Thai Buddhist religion, which forbids the killing of animals, most butchers in Thailand are immigrant workers, such as the Chinese. Religion does not forbid eating meat, although it is often regarded as a special treat. Chicken is much more common than beef, and it's not unusual to see chicken, or sometimes pork, combined with seafood such as prawns or crab meat – a combination which works surprisingly well. Duck, another Thai favourite, is frequently barbecue-roasted with warm spices and soy or sweet glazes, much as in the Chinese style.

Stir-fried Beef with Beansprouts

Serves 4

INGREDIENTS

1 bunch spring onions
2 tbsp sunflower oil
1 garlic clove, crushed
1 tsp finely chopped fresh
    root ginger
500 g/1 lb 2 oz tender beef, cut
    into thin strips

1 large red pepper, deseeded
    and sliced
1 small fresh red chilli, deseeded
    and chopped
350 g/12 oz fresh beansprouts
1 small lemon grass stalk,
    finely chopped
2 tbsp smooth peanut butter

4 tbsp coconut milk
1 tbsp rice vinegar
1 tbsp soy sauce
1 tsp soft light brown sugar
250 g/9 oz medium egg noodles
salt and pepper

1 Trim and thinly slice the spring onions, reserving a few slices to use as a garnish.

2 Heat the oil in a frying pan or wok over a high heat. Add the spring onions, garlic and ginger and stir-fry for 2–3 minutes to soften. Add the beef and continue stir-frying for 4–5 minutes until browned evenly.

3 Add the pepper and stir-fry for 3–4 minutes. Add

the chilli and beansprouts and stir-fry for a further 2 minutes.

4 Mix together the lemon grass, peanut butter, coconut milk, vinegar, soy sauce and sugar, then stir this mixture into the wok.

5 Meanwhile, cook the egg noodles in boiling, lightly salted water for 4 minutes, or according to the packet instructions. Drain

thoroughly and stir into the frying pan or wok, tossing to mix evenly.

6 Adjust seasoning with salt and pepper to taste. Sprinkle with the reserved spring onions and serve hot.

Beef Satay with Peanut Sauce

Serves 4

INGREDIENTS

500 g/1 lb 2 oz beef fillet
2 garlic cloves, crushed
2 cm/¾ in piece fresh root ginger,
    finely grated
1 tbsp soft light brown sugar
1 tbsp dark soy sauce
1 tbsp lime juice
2 tsp sesame oil

1 tsp ground coriander
1 tsp turmeric
½ tsp chilli powder
chopped cucumber and red
    pepper, to serve

PEANUT SAUCE
300 ml/10 fl oz coconut milk
8 tbsp crunchy peanut butter
½ small onion, grated
2 tsp soft light brown sugar
½ tsp chilli powder
1 tbsp dark soy sauce

1 Cut the beef into 1 cm/ ½ inch cubes and place in a large bowl.

2 Add the garlic, ginger, sugar, soy sauce, lime juice, sesame oil, ground coriander, turmeric and chilli powder. Mix well to coat the pieces of meat evenly. Cover and leave to marinate in the refrigerator for at least 2 hours, or overnight.

3 To make the peanut sauce, place all the ingredients in a saucepan and stir over a medium heat until boiling. Remove from the heat and keep warm.

4 Thread the beef cubes on to bamboo skewers. Grill the skewers under a preheated grill, turning frequently, for 3–5 minutes until golden. Alternatively, barbecue the skewers over hot coals. Serve with the peanut sauce and chopped cucumber and red pepper pieces as garnish.

COOK'S TIP

Cook the tender beef very quickly on a high heat, sealing in all the juices and flavour. Make sure the grill or barbecue is very hot before you start to cook. Soak the skewers in cold water for about 20 minutes before threading the meat on to them – this reduces the risk of the skewers burning.

Beef & Peppers with Lemon Grass

Serves 4

INGREDIENTS

500 g/1 lb 2 oz lean beef fillet
2 tbsp vegetable oil
1 garlic clove, finely chopped
1 lemon grass stalk,
    finely shredded

2.5 cm/1 in piece fresh root
    ginger, finely chopped
1 red pepper, deseeded and
    thickly sliced

1 green pepper, deseeded and
    thickly sliced
1 onion, thickly sliced
2 tbsp lime juice
boiled noodles or rice, to serve

1 Cut the beef into long, thin strips, cutting it across the grain.

2 Heat the oil in a large, heavy-based frying pan or wok over a high heat. Add the garlic and stir-fry for 1 minute.

3 Add the beef and stir-fry for a further 2–3 minutes until lightly coloured. Stir in the lemon grass and ginger and remove the pan or wok from the heat.

4 Remove the beef from the pan or wok and keep to one side. Next add the peppers and onion to the pan or wok and stir-fry over a high heat for 2–3 minutes until the onions are just turning golden brown and slightly softened.

5 Return the beef to the pan, stir in the lime juice and season to taste with salt and pepper. Serve with noodles or rice.

COOK'S TIP

When preparing lemon grass, take care to remove the outer layers which can be tough and fibrous. Use only the centre, tender part, which has the finest flavour.

Pork with Soy & Sesame Glaze

Serves 4

INGREDIENTS

2 pork fillets, about 275 g/
  9½ oz each
2 tbsp dark soy sauce
2 tbsp clear honey

2 garlic cloves, crushed
1 tbsp sesame seeds
1 onion, thinly sliced in rings

1 tbsp seasoned plain flour
sunflower oil, for frying
crisp salad, to serve

1 Trim the pork fillets and place them in a wide non-metallic dish.

2 Mix together the soy sauce, honey and garlic. Spread this mixture over the pork, turning the meat to coat it evenly.

3 Lift the pork fillets into a roasting tin or shallow ovenproof dish. Sprinkle evenly with sesame seeds.

4 Roast the pork in a preheated oven, 200°C/400°F/ Gas Mark 6, for about 20 minutes, spooning over any juices. Cover loosely with foil to prevent over-browning and roast for a further 10–15 minutes until the meat is thoroughly cooked and tender.

5 Meanwhile, dip the onion slices in the flour and shake off the excess. Heat the oil and fry the onion rings until golden and crisp, turning occasionally. Serve the pork in slices with the fried onions on a bed of crisp salad.

COOK'S TIP

This pork is also excellent served cold, and it's a good choice for picnics, especially served with a spicy sambal (see page 162) or chilli relish.

Stir-fried Pork and Corn

Serves 4

INGREDIENTS

2 tbsp vegetable oil
500 g/1 lb 2 oz lean boneless
    pork, cut in thin strips
1 garlic clove, chopped
350 g/12 oz fresh
    sweetcorn kernels

200 g/7 oz French beans, cut into
    short lengths
2 spring onions, chopped
1 small fresh red chilli, chopped

1 tsp sugar
1 tbsp light soy sauce
3 tbsp chopped fresh coriander
egg noodles or boiled rice,
    to serve

1 Heat the oil in a large, heavy-based frying pan or wok and stir-fry the pork quickly over a high heat until lightly browned.

2 Stir in the garlic, sweetcorn, beans, spring onions and chilli and continue stir-frying over a high heat for 2–3 minutes, until the vegetables are heated through and almost tender.

3 Stir in the sugar and soy sauce and stir-fry for a further 30 seconds over a high heat.

4 Sprinkle with the chopped coriander and serve immediately either with egg noodles or rice.

COOK'S TIP

In Thailand, long beans would be used for dishes such as this, but you can substitute French beans, which are more easily available. But look out for long beans in Oriental food stores – they are like long string beans and have a similar flavour, but their texture is crisp and they cook more quickly.

Spicy Fried Minced Pork

Serves 4

INGREDIENTS

2 garlic cloves

3 shallots

2.5 cm/1 in piece fresh root
  ginger, finely chopped

2 tbsp sunflower oil

500 g/1 lb 2 oz lean minced pork

2 tbsp Thai fish sauce

1 tbsp dark soy sauce

1 tbsp Thai red curry paste

4 dried kaffir lime
  leaves, crumbled

4 plum tomatoes, chopped

3 tbsp chopped fresh coriander

salt and pepper

fresh coriander sprigs,
  to garnish

boiled fine egg noodles, to serve

1 Finely chop the garlic, shallots and ginger. Heat the oil in a wok over a medium heat. Add the garlic, shallots and ginger and stir-fry for about 2 minutes. Stir in the minced pork and continue stir-frying until golden brown.

2 Stir in the fish sauce, soy sauce, curry paste and lime leaves, and stir-fry for a further 1–2 minutes over a high heat.

3 Add the chopped tomatoes and cook, stirring occasionally, for a further 5–6 minutes.

4 Stir in the chopped coriander and season to taste with salt and pepper. Serve hot, spooned on to a bed of boiled fine egg noodles, garnished with coriander sprigs.

COOK'S TIP

Dried kaffir lime leaves are a useful store-cupboard ingredient as they can be crumbled easily straight into quick dishes such as this. If you prefer to use fresh kaffir lime leaves, shred them finely and add to the dish.

Thai-spiced Sausages

Serves 4

INGREDIENTS

400 g/14 oz lean minced pork	1 tsp ground coriander	2 tbsp chopped fresh coriander
4 tbsp cooked rice	½ tsp salt	3 tbsp groundnut oil
1 garlic clove, crushed	3 tbsp lime juice	coconut sambal or soy sauce,
1 tsp Thai red curry paste		to serve
1 tsp pepper		

1 Place the pork, rice, garlic, curry paste, pepper, ground coriander, salt, lime juice and chopped coriander in a bowl and knead together with your hands to mix evenly.

2 Use your hands to shape the mixture into 12 small sausage shapes. If you can buy sausage casings, fill the casings and twist at intervals to separate the sausages.

3 Heat the oil in a large frying pan over a medium heat. Add the sausages, in batches if necessary, and fry for

8–10 minutes, turning them over occasionally, until they are evenly golden brown. Serve hot with a coconut sambal or soy sauce.

COOK'S TIP

These sausages can also be served as a starter – shape the mixture slightly smaller to make about 16 bite-size sausages. Serve with a soy dip.

Thai-style Burgers

Serves 4

INGREDIENTS

1 small lemon grass stalk
1 small fresh red chilli, deseeded
2 garlic cloves, peeled
2 spring onions
200 g/7 oz closed-
    cup mushrooms

400 g/14 oz minced pork
1 tbsp Thai fish sauce
3 tbsp chopped fresh coriander
sunflower oil, for frying
2 tbsp mayonnaise
1 tbsp lime juice
salt and pepper

TO SERVE
4 sesame hamburger buns
shredded Chinese leaves

1 Place the lemon grass stalk, chilli, garlic and spring onions in a food processor and process to a smooth paste.

2 Add the mushrooms and process until very finely chopped and mixed in.

3 Add the minced pork, fish sauce and coriander. Season well with salt and pepper, then divide the mixture into 4 equal portions and, with lightly floured hands, shape them into flat burger shapes.

4 Heat the oil in a frying pan over a medium heat. Add the burgers and fry gently for 6–8 minutes until done or as you like.

5 Meanwhile, mix the mayonnaise with the lime juice. Split the hamburger buns and spread the lime-flavoured mayonnaise on the cut surfaces. Add a few shredded Chinese leaves, top with a burger and sandwich together. Serve immediately, while still hot.

COOK'S TIP

You can add a spoonful of your favourite relish to each burger, or alternatively, add a few pieces of crisp pickled vegetables for a change of texture (see page 160).

Red Lamb Curry

Serves 4

INGREDIENTS

500 g/1 lb 2 oz boneless lean leg
  of lamb
2 tbsp vegetable oil
1 large onion, sliced
2 garlic cloves, crushed
2 tbsp Thai red curry paste
150 ml/5 fl oz coconut milk
1 tbsp soft light brown sugar

1 large red pepper, deseeded and
  thickly sliced
120 ml/4 fl oz lamb or beef stock
1 tbsp Thai fish sauce
2 tbsp lime juice
227 g/8 oz can water
  chestnuts, drained
2 tbsp chopped fresh coriander

2 tbsp chopped fresh basil
salt and pepper
fresh basil leaves, to garnish
boiled jasmine rice, to serve

1 Trim the meat and cut it into 3 cm/1¼ inch cubes. Heat the oil in a large, heavy-based frying pan or wok over a high heat. Add the onion and garlic and stir-fry for 2–3 minutes to soften. Add the cubes of lamb and stir-fry the mixture quickly until lightly browned.

2 Stir in the red curry paste and cook for a few seconds, then add the coconut milk and sugar and bring to the boil. Reduce the heat and simmer gently, stirring occasionally, for 15 minutes.

3 Stir in the red pepper, stock, fish sauce and lime juice, cover and continue simmering for a further 15 minutes or until the meat is tender.

4 Add the water chestnuts, coriander and basil and adjust the seasoning to taste with salt and pepper. Serve the curry immediately with jasmine rice garnished with fresh basil leaves.

COOK'S TIP

This curry can also be made with other lean red meats. Try replacing the lamb with trimmed duck breasts or pieces of lean braising beef.

Roast Chicken with Ginger & Lime

Serves 4

INGREDIENTS

3 cm/1¼ inch piece fresh root ginger, finely chopped
2 garlic cloves, finely chopped
1 lemon grass stalk, finely chopped

1 small onion, finely chopped
½ tsp salt
1 tsp black peppercorns
1.5 kg/3 lb 5 oz roasting chicken
1 tbsp coconut cream

2 tbsp lime juice
2 tbsp clear honey
1 tsp cornflour
2 tsp water
stir-fried vegetables, to serve

1 Put the ginger, garlic, lemon grass, onion, salt and peppercorns in a mortar and and crush with a pestle to form a smooth paste.

2 Cut the chicken in half lengthways, using poultry shears or strong kitchen scissors. Spread the paste all over the chicken, both inside and out, and spread it on to the flesh under the breast skin. Cover and chill overnight or at least for several hours.

3 In a small pan, heat the coconut cream, lime juice and honey together, stirring until smooth. Brush a little of the mixture evenly over the chicken.

4 Place the chicken halves on a tray over a roasting tin half-filled with boiling water. Roast in a preheated oven, 180°C/ 350°F/Gas Mark 4, basting occasionally with the reserved lime and honey mixture, for about 1 hour or until the chicken is a rich golden brown.

5 When the chicken is cooked, boil the water from the roasting tin to reduce it to about 100 ml/ 3½ fl oz. Blend the cornflour and water to a smooth paste and stir into the reduced liquid. Bring to the boil over a low heat, then stir until slightly thickened and clear. Serve the chicken with the sauce and a selection of stir-fried vegetables.

Chicken & Mango Stir-fry

Serves 4

INGREDIENTS

6 boneless, skinless
chicken thighs
2.5 cm/1 inch piece fresh root
ginger, grated
1 garlic clove, crushed
1 small fresh red chilli, deseeded
1 large red pepper

4 spring onions
200 g/7 oz mangetouts
100 g/3½ oz baby sweetcorn cobs
1 large, firm, ripe mango
2 tbsp sunflower oil
1 tbsp light soy sauce
3 tbsp rice wine or sherry

1 tsp sesame oil
salt and pepper
sliced chives, to garnish

1 Cut the chicken into long, thin strips and place in a bowl. Mix together the ginger, garlic and chilli, then stir into the chicken strips to coat them evenly.

2 Slice the pepper thinly, cutting diagonally. Trim and diagonally slice the spring onions. Cut the mangetouts and baby sweetcorn in half diagonally. Peel the mango and slice thinly, cutting the flesh away from the central stone.

3 Heat the oil in a large, heavy-based frying pan or wok over a high heat. Add the chicken and stir-fry for 4–5 minutes until just turning golden brown.

4 Add the peppers and stir-fry over a medium heat for 4–5 minutes until softened.

5 Add the spring onions, mangetouts and baby sweetcorn and stir-fry for a further minute.

6 Mix together the soy sauce, rice wine or sherry and sesame oil and stir the mixture into the wok or pan. Add the mango and stir gently for 1 minute to heat thoroughly.

7 Adjust the seasoning with salt and pepper to taste and serve immediately, garnished with chives.

Thai-spiced Coriander Chicken

Serves 4

INGREDIENTS

4 skinless boneless
    chicken breasts
2 garlic cloves, peeled
1 fresh green chilli, deseeded
2 cm/¾ inch piece fresh root
    ginger, peeled

4 tbsp chopped fresh coriander
finely grated rind of 1 lime
3 tbsp lime juice
2 tbsp light soy sauce
1 tbsp caster sugar
175 ml/6 fl oz coconut milk

cucumber and radish slices,
    to garnish
plain boiled rice, to serve

1 Using a sharp knife, cut 3 deep slashes into the skinned side of each chicken breast. Arrange the chicken breasts in a single layer in a large, wide glass or earthenware dish.

2 Put the garlic, chilli, ginger, chopped coriander, lime rind, lime juice, soy sauce, caster sugar and coconut milk in a food processor and process until a smooth purée forms.

3 Spread the purée over both sides of the chicken breasts, coating them evenly. Cover the dish with clingfilm and set aside to marinate in the refrigerator for at least 1 hour.

4 Lift the chicken from the marinade, drain off the excess and place in a grill pan. Grill under a preheated medium grill for about 12–15 minutes until evenly cooked through.

5 Meanwhile, place the remaining marinade in a saucepan and bring to the boil. Lower the heat and simmer for several minutes to heat thoroughly. Serve with the chicken breasts, garnished with cucumber and radish slices, and accompanied with rice.

Green Chicken Curry

Serves 4

INGREDIENTS

6 boneless, skinless
    chicken thighs
400 ml/14 fl oz coconut milk
2 garlic cloves, crushed
2 tbsp Thai fish sauce

2 tbsp Thai green curry paste
12 baby aubergines, also called
    Thai pea aubergines
3 fresh green chillies,
    finely chopped

3 kaffir lime leaves, shredded
4 tbsp chopped fresh coriander
boiled rice, to serve

1 Cut the chicken into bite-size pieces. Pour the coconut milk into a large pan or wok and bring to the boil over a high heat.

2 Add the chicken, garlic and fish sauce to the pan and bring back to the boil. Lower the heat and simmer gently for 30 minutes, or until the chicken is just tender and cooked through.

3 Remove the chicken from the mixture with a perforated spoon. Set aside and keep warm.

4 Stir the green curry paste into the pan, add the aubergines, chillies and lime leaves and simmer gently for 5 minutes.

5 Return the chicken to the pan and bring to the boil. Adjust the seasoning to taste with salt and pepper, then stir in the coriander. Serve the curry hot with boiled rice.

COOK'S TIP

Baby aubergines or 'pea aubergines', as they are called in Thailand, are traditionally used in this curry, but they are not always easily available outside the country. If you can't find them in an Oriental food shop, use chopped ordinary aubergine or substitute a few green peas.

Braised Chicken with Garlic & Spices

Serves 4

INGREDIENTS

4 garlic cloves, chopped

4 shallots, chopped

2 small fresh red chillies, deseeded and chopped

1 lemon grass stalk, finely chopped

1 tbsp chopped fresh coriander

1 tsp shrimp paste

½ tsp ground cinnamon

1 tbsp tamarind paste

2 tbsp vegetable oil

8 small chicken joints, such as drumsticks or thighs

300 ml/10 fl oz chicken stock

1 tbsp Thai fish sauce

1 tbsp smooth peanut butter

salt and pepper

4 tbsp toasted peanuts, chopped

TO SERVE

stir-fried vegetables

boiled noodles

1 Place the garlic, shallots, chillies, lemon grass, coriander and shrimp paste in a mortar and grind to an almost smooth paste with a pestle. Add the ground cinnamon and tamarind paste to the mixture.

2 Heat the oil in a wide frying pan or wok. Add the chicken joints and cook, turning frequently, until they are golden brown on all sides. Remove them from the wok and keep hot. Tip away any excess fat.

3 Add the spice paste to the pan or wok and stir over a medium heat until lightly browned. Stir in the chicken stock and return the chicken to the pan.

4 Bring to the boil, then cover tightly, lower the heat and simmer for about 25–30 minutes, stirring occasionally, until the chicken is tender and cooked through. Stir in the fish sauce and peanut butter and simmer the mixture gently for a further 10 minutes.

5 Adjust the seasoning with salt and pepper to taste and scatter the toasted peanuts over the chicken. Serve hot, with a colourful selection of stir-fry vegetables and boiled noodles.

Duck Breasts with Chilli & Lime

Serves 4

INGREDIENTS

4 boneless duck breasts	1 tbsp soy sauce	120 ml/4 fl oz chicken stock
2 garlic cloves, crushed	1 tsp chilli sauce	salt and pepper
4 tsp light soft brown sugar	1 tsp vegetable oil	
3 tbsp lime juice	2 tbsp plum jam	

1 Using a small, sharp knife, cut deep slashes in the skin of the duck to make a diamond pattern. Arrange the duck breasts, in a single layer, a wide glass or earthenware dish.

2 Mix together the garlic, sugar, lime juice, soy and chilli sauces in a small bowl, then spoon over the duck breasts, turning well to coat them evenly.

3 Cover the dish with clingfilm and set aside to marinate in the refrigerator for at least 3 hours or, preferably, overnight.

4 Drain the duck, reserving the marinade. Heat a large, heavy-based pan until very hot and brush with the oil. Add the duck breasts, skin side down, and cook for about 5 minutes or until the skin is browned and crisp. Tip away the excess fat. Turn the duck breasts over.

5 Continue cooking on the other side for 2–3 minutes to brown. Add the reserved marinade, plum jam and stock and simmer for 2 minutes. Adjust the seasoning to taste and serve hot, with the juices spooned over.

COOK'S TIP

If you prefer to reduce the overall fat content of this dish, remove the skin from the duck breasts before cooking and reduce the cooking time slightly.

Roasted Duck Curried with Pineapple & Coconut

Serves 4

INGREDIENTS

1.6 kg/3½ lb duckling	½ tsp ground coriander	TO GARNISH
2 tbsp groundnut oil	1 tbsp Thai green curry paste	chopped fresh coriander
1 small pineapple	1 tsp soft light brown sugar	fresh red chilli strips
1 large onion, chopped	450 ml/16 fl oz coconut milk	
1 garlic clove, finely chopped	salt and pepper	
1 tsp finely chopped fresh	boiled jasmine rice, to serve	
root ginger		

1 Using a large knife or poultry shears, cut the duck in half lengthways, cutting through the line of the breastbone. Wipe inside and out with paper towels. Sprinkle with salt and pepper, prick the skin with a fork and brush with oil.

2 Place the duck, cut side down, on a grill pan and grill under a preheated hot grill for 25–30 minutes, turning occasionally, until golden brown all over. Tip away the fat in the pan, as it may catch fire.

3 Allow the duck to cool, then cut each half into 2 portions. Peel and core the pineapple, then cut the flesh into dice shapes.

4 Heat the remaining oil in a large, heavy-based pan and fry the onion and garlic for 3–4 minutes over a low heat until softened. Stir in the ginger, ground coriander, curry paste and brown sugar and stir-fry for 1 minute.

5 Stir in the coconut milk and bring to the boil. Add the duck pieces and the pineapple. Reduce the heat and simmer for 5 minutes. Serve immediately, sprinkled with chopped coriander and chilli strips, accompanied with boiled jasmine rice.

Steamed Yellow Fish Fillets

Serves 4

INGREDIENTS

500 g/1 lb 2 oz firm fish fillets,
    such as red snapper, sole
    or monkfish
1 dried red bird-eye chilli
1 small onion, chopped
3 garlic cloves, chopped

2 fresh coriander sprigs
1 tsp coriander seeds
½ tsp ground turmeric
½ tsp pepper
1 tbsp Thai fish sauce
2 tbsp coconut milk

1 small egg, lightly beaten
2 tbsp rice flour
fresh red and green chilli strips,
    to garnish
soy sauce, to serve

1 Remove any skin from the fish and membrane from monkfish, if using, and cut the fillets diagonally into long 2 cm/¾ inch wide strips.

2 Place the dried chilli, onion, garlic, coriander and coriander seeds in a mortar and grind to a smooth paste with a pestle.

3 Add the turmeric, pepper, fish sauce, coconut milk and beaten egg, stirring well to mix evenly.

4 Dip the fish strips into the paste mixture, then into the rice flour to coat lightly and evenly.

5 Bring the water in the bottom of a steamer to the boil, then arrange the fish strips in the top of the steamer. Cover and steam for about 12–15 minutes until the fish is just firm.

6 Serve the fish hot, garnished with red and green chilli strips and hand the soy sauce separately.

COOK'S TIP

If you don't have a steamer, improvise by placing a large metal colander over a large pan of boiling water and cover with an upturned plate to enclose the fish as it steams.

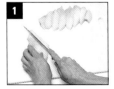

Baked Fish with Pepper, Chillies & Basil

Serves 4

INGREDIENTS

handful of fresh sweet basil leaves
750 g/1 lb 10 oz whole red
    snapper, sea bass or John
    Dory, cleaned
2 tbsp groundnut oil
2 tbsp Thai fish sauce

2 garlic cloves, crushed
1 tsp finely grated galangal or
    root ginger
2 large fresh red chillies,
    sliced diagonally

1 yellow pepper, deseeded
    and diced
1 tbsp palm sugar
1 tbsp rice vinegar
2 tbsp water or fish stock
2 tomatoes, deseeded and sliced

1 Reserve a few fresh basil leaves for garnish and tuck the rest inside the body cavity of the fish.

2 Heat 1 tablespoon of the oil in a wide frying pan and fry the fish quickly to brown, turning once. Place the fish on a large piece of foil in a roasting tin and spoon over the fish sauce. Wrap the foil over the fish loosely and bake in a preheated oven, 190°C/375°F/Gas Mark 5, for 25–30 minutes until just cooked though.

3 Meanwhile, heat the remaining oil and fry the garlic, galangal or ginger and chillies for 30 seconds. Add the pepper and stir-fry for a further 2–3 minutes to soften.

4 Stir in the sugar, rice vinegar and water, then add the tomatoes and bring to the boil. Remove the pan from the heat.

5 Remove the fish from the oven and transfer to a warmed serving plate. Add the fish juices to the pan,

then spoon the sauce over the fish and scatter with the reserved basil leaves. Serve the fish immediately.

COOK'S TIP

Large red chillies are less hot than the tiny red bird-eye chillies, so you can use them more freely in cooked dishes such as this for a mild heat. Remove the seeds if you prefer.

Baked Cod with a Curry Crust

Serves 4

INGREDIENTS

½ tsp sesame oil
4 pieces cod fillet, about
150 g/5½ oz each
85 g/3 oz fresh
white breadcrumbs

2 tbsp chopped
blanched almonds
2 tsp Thai green curry paste
finely grated rind of ½ lime
salt and pepper

boiled new potatoes, to serve
lime slices and rind and mixed
green leaves, to garnish

1 Brush the sesame oil over the base of a wide, shallow ovenproof dish or tin, then place the pieces of cod in a single layer.

2 Mix together the fresh breadcrumbs, almonds, curry paste and grated lime rind, stirring well to blend thoroughly and evenly. Season to taste with salt and pepper.

3 Carefully spoon the crumb mixture over the fish pieces, pressing lightly to hold it in place.

4 Place the dish, uncovered, in a preheated oven, 200°C/400°F/Gas Mark 6, and bake for 35–40 minutes until the fish is cooked through and tender and the crumb topping is golden brown.

5 Serve the dish hot, garnished with lime slices and rind and mixed green leaves and accompanied with boiled new potatoes.

COOK'S TIP

To test whether the fish is cooked through, use a fork to pierce it in the thickest part – if the flesh is white all the way through and flakes apart easily, it is cooked sufficiently.

Whole Fried Fish with Soy & Ginger

Serves 4–6

INGREDIENTS

6 dried Chinese mushrooms

3 tbsp rice vinegar

2 tbsp soft light brown sugar

3 tbsp dark soy sauce

7.5 cm/3 inch piece fresh root
    ginger, finely chopped

4 spring onions, sliced diagonally

2 tsp cornflour

2 tbsp lime juice

1 sea bass, about 1 kg/
    2 lb 4 oz, cleaned

4 tbsp plain flour

sunflower oil, for deep-frying

salt and pepper

1 radish, sliced but left whole,
    to garnish

shredded Chinese leaves and
    radish slices, to serve

1 Soak the dried mushrooms in hot water for about 10 minutes, then drain well, reserving 100 ml/3½ fl oz of the liquid. Cut the mushrooms into thin slices.

2 Mix the reserved mushroom liquid with the rice vinegar, sugar and soy sauce. Place in a saucepan with the mushrooms and bring to the boil. Reduce the heat and simmer for 3–4 minutes.

3 Add the ginger and spring onions and simmer for 1 minute. Blend the cornflour and lime juice together to a smooth paste, stir into the pan and stir for 1–2 minutes until the sauce thickens and clears. Keep the sauce to one side while you cook the fish.

4 Season the fish inside and out with salt and pepper, then dust lightly with flour, carefully shaking off the excess.

5 Heat a 2.5 cm/1 inch depth of oil in a wide pan to 190°C/375°F or until a cube of bread browns in 30 seconds. Carefully lower the fish into the oil and fry on one side for about 3–4 minutes until golden. Use 2 metal spatulas or fish slices to turn the fish carefully and then fry on the other side for a further 3–4 minutes until golden.

6 Lift the fish out of the pan, draining off the excess oil, and place on a serving plate. Heat the sauce until boiling, then spoon it over the fish. Serve hot, garnished with the sliced whole radish, surrounded by shredded Chinese leaves with sliced radishes.

Spiced Tuna in Sweet-and-Sour Sauce

Serves 4

INGREDIENTS

4 fresh tuna steaks, about
    500 g/1 lb 2 oz total weight
¼ tsp pepper
2 tbsp groundnut oil
1 onion, diced
1 small red pepper, deseeded and
    cut into matchsticks
1 garlic clove, crushed

½ cucumber, deseeded and cut
    into matchsticks
2 pineapple slices, diced
1 tsp finely chopped fresh
    root ginger
1 tbsp soft light brown sugar
1 tbsp cornflour
4½ tsp lime juice

1 tbsp Thai fish sauce
250 ml/9 fl oz fish stock

TO GARNISH
lime slices
cucumber slices

1 Sprinkle the tuna steaks with pepper on both sides. Heat a heavy frying pan or griddle and brush with a little of the oil. Arrange the tuna steaks in the pan or on the griddle and cook for about 8 minutes, turning them over once.

2 Heat the remaining oil in another pan and fry the onion, red pepper and garlic over a low heat for 3–4 minutes to soften.

3 Remove the pan from the heat and stir in the cucumber, pineapple, ginger and sugar.

4 Blend the cornflour with the lime juice and fish sauce to a smooth paste, then stir into the stock and add to the pan. Stir over a medium heat until boiling, then cook for 1–2 minutes until the sauce is thickened and clear.

5 Spoon the sauce over the tuna and serve garnished with lime slices and cucumber.

COOK'S TIP

Tuna can be served quite lightly cooked, and can be dry if it is overcooked.

Thai-spiced Salmon

Serves 4

INGREDIENTS

2.5 cm/1 in piece fresh root
    ginger, grated
1 tsp coriander seeds, crushed
¼ tsp chilli powder

1 tbsp lime juice
1 tsp sesame oil
4 pieces salmon fillet with skin,
    about 150 g/5½ oz each

2 tbsp vegetable oil
boiled rice and stir-fried
    vegetables, to serve

1 Mix together the grated ginger, crushed coriander, chilli powder, lime juice and sesame oil.

2 Place the salmon on a wide, non-metallic plate or dish and spoon the mixture over the flesh side of the fillets, spreading it to coat each piece of salmon evenly.

3 Cover the dish with cling film and chill the salmon in the refrigerator for about 30 minutes.

4 Heat a wide, heavy-based frying pan or griddle pan with the oil over a high heat.

Place the salmon in the hot pan or on the griddle, skin side down.

5 Cook the salmon for 4–5 minutes, without turning, until it is crusty underneath and the flesh flakes easily. Serve at once with the boiled rice and stir-fried vegetables.

COOK'S TIP

It's important to use a heavy-based pan or solid griddle for this recipe, so the fish cooks evenly throughout without sticking. If the fish is very thick, you may prefer to turn it over carefully to cook on the other side for 2–3 minutes.

Salmon with Red Curry in Banana Leaves

Serves 4

INGREDIENTS

4 salmon steaks, about 175 g/
  6 oz each
2 banana leaves, halved
1 garlic clove, crushed
1 tsp grated fresh root ginger

1 tbsp Thai red curry paste
1 tsp soft light brown sugar
1 tbsp Thai fish sauce
2 tbsp lime juice

TO GARNISH
lime wedges
finely chopped fresh red chilli

1 Place a salmon steak on the centre of each half banana leaf.

2 Mix together the garlic, ginger, curry paste, sugar and fish sauce. Spread this mixture over the surface of the fish and sprinkle with lime juice.

3 Wrap the banana leaves around the fish, tucking in the sides as you go to make a neat bundle.

4 Place the parcels seam side down on a baking tray and bake in a preheated oven, 220°C/425°F/Gas Mark 7, for 15–20 minutes until the fish is cooked and the banana leaves are beginning to brown. Serve garnished with lime wedges and chopped chilli.

COOK'S TIP

Fresh banana leaves are often sold in packs containing several leaves, but if you buy more than you need, they will store in the refrigerator for about a week.

Spicy Thai Seafood Stew

Serves 4

INGREDIENTS

200 g/7 oz squid, cleaned
500 g/1 lb 2 oz firm white fish
    fillet, preferably monkfish
    or halibut
1 tbsp sunflower oil
4 shallots, finely chopped
2 garlic cloves, finely chopped

2 tbsp green Thai curry paste
2 small lemon grass stalks,
    finely chopped
1 tsp shrimp paste
500 ml/18 fl oz coconut milk
200 g/7 oz raw tiger prawns,
    peeled and de-veined

12 fresh clams in shells, cleaned
8 fresh basil leaves,
    finely shredded
fresh basil leaves, to garnish
boiled rice, to serve

1 Cut the squid body cavities into thick rings, and the fish fillet into bite-sized chunks.

2 Heat the oil in a large frying pan or wok and stir-fry the shallots, garlic and curry paste for 1–2 minutes. Add the lemon grass and shrimp paste, stir in the coconut milk and bring to the boil.

3 Reduce the heat until the liquid is simmering gently, then add the white fish, squid and prawns to the pan and simmer gently for 2 minutes.

4 Add the clams and simmer for a further minute until the clams open. Discard any clams that do not open.

5 Scatter the shredded basil leaves over the stew, and serve immediately, garnished with whole basil leaves and spooned over boiled rice.

COOK'S TIP

If you prefer, fresh mussels in shells can be used instead of clams – add them in Step 4 and follow the recipe.

Stir-fried Squid with Hot Black Bean Sauce

Serves 4

INGREDIENTS

750 g/1 lb 10 oz squid, cleaned
1 large red pepper, deseeded
85 g/3 oz mangetouts, trimmed
1 head pak choi
3 tbsp black bean sauce
1 tbsp Thai fish sauce
1 tbsp rice wine

1 tbsp dark soy sauce
1 tsp soft light brown sugar
1 tsp cornflour
1 tbsp water
1 tbsp sunflower oil
1 tsp sesame oil

1 small fresh red bird's-eye chilli, chopped
1 garlic clove, finely chopped
1 tsp grated fresh root ginger
2 spring onions, chopped

1 Cut the tentacles from the squid and discard. Cut the body cavities into quarters lengthways. Use the tip of a small sharp knife to score a diamond pattern into the flesh, without cutting all the way through. Pat dry with kitchen paper.

2 Cut the pepper into long, thin slices. Cut the mangetouts in half diagonally. Coarsely shred the pak choi.

3 Mix together the black bean sauce, fish sauce, rice wine, soy sauce and sugar. Blend the cornflour with the water to a smooth paste and stir into the other sauce ingredients. Keep to one side.

4 Heat the oils in a wok. Add the chilli, garlic, ginger and spring onions and stir-fry for about 1 minute. Add the pepper and stir-fry for about 2 minutes.

5 Add the squid and stir-fry over a high heat for a further minute. Stir in the mangetouts and pak choi, and stir for a further minute until wilted.

6 Stir in the sauce ingredients and cook, stirring, for about 2 minutes, until the sauce clears and thickens. Serve immediately.

Spicy Scallops with Lime & Chilli

Serves 4

INGREDIENTS

16 large scallops
1 tbsp butter
1 tbsp vegetable oil
1 tsp crushed garlic
1 tsp grated fresh root ginger

1 bunch spring onions,
    finely sliced
rind of 1 kaffir lime, finely grated
1 small fresh red chilli, deseeded
    and very finely chopped

3 tbsp kaffir lime juice
salt and pepper
lime wedges and boiled rice,
    to serve

1 Trim the scallops to remove any black intestine, then wash and pat dry with kitchen paper. Separate the corals from the white parts, then horizontally slice each white part in half, making 2 rounds.

2 Heat the butter and oil in a frying pan or wok. Add the garlic and ginger and stir-fry for 1 minute without browning. Add the spring onions and stir-fry for a further minute.

3 Add the scallops and continue stir-frying over a high heat for 4–5 minutes. Stir in the lime rind, chilli and lime juice and cook for a further minute.

4 Serve the scallops hot, with the juices spooned over them, accompanied by lime wedges and boiled rice.

COOK'S TIP

If fresh scallops are not available, frozen ones can be used, but make sure they are thoroughly defrosted before you cook them. Drain off all excess moisture and pat dry with kitchen paper.

Prawn Skewers with Chilli & Tamarind Glaze

Serves 4

INGREDIENTS

1 garlic clove, chopped

1 fresh red bird-eye chilli,
    deseeded and chopped

1 tbsp tamarind paste

1 tbsp sesame oil

1 tbsp dark soy sauce

2 tbsp lime juice

1 tbsp soft light brown sugar

16 large raw tiger prawns,
    shells on

TO SERVE

lime wedges

crusty bread

salad leaves

1 Put the garlic, chilli, tamarind, sesame oil, soy sauce, lime juice and sugar in a small pan. Stir over a low heat until the sugar is dissolved, then remove from the heat and allow to cool completely.

2 Wash the prawns, pat dry with kitchen paper and place in a single layer in a wide, non-metallic dish. Spoon the marinade over the prawns and turn them over to coat evenly. Cover the dish with clingfilm and leave in the refrigerator to

marinate for at least 2 hours or, preferably, overnight.

3 Meanwhile, soak 4 bamboo or wooden skewers in water for about 20 minutes. Drain and thread 4 prawns on to each skewer.

4 Grill the skewers under a preheated hot grill for 5–6 minutes, turning them over once, until the prawns turn pink and begin to brown. Alternatively, barbecue the skewers over hot coals.

5 Thread a wedge of lime on to the end of each skewer and serve with crusty bread and salad leaves.

Noodles & Rice

With its monsoon climate and abundant rainfall, Thailand has the ideal conditions for rice growing and has become one of the major rice producers in the world. It's thought that rice grew there as far back as 3500 BC. So, not surprisingly, rice is the main staple food in Thailand and hardly a meal goes by without it appearing in some form or another.

Two main varieties of rice are used in Thai cooking – a long and a short grain. The long grain is Thai fragrant rice, a good-quality white, fluffy rice with delicately scented, separate grains. Glutinous or 'sticky' rice is a round grain rice with a high starch content which causes the grains to stick together.

Noodles also play a vital part in Thai meals and street vendors serve them as a snack at all times of day. Rice noodles in flat ribbons or thin vermicelli are the most common, and these need to be soaked before being fried or added to soups and stir-fries. Cellophane noodles are also locally made, but egg noodles are often imported from China. Most noodle dishes are served with an array of condiments for the diner to add to his or her taste – usually including crushed dried chillies, finely chopped peanuts, Thai fish sauce, soy sauce and sugar.

Crispy Rice Noodles

Serves 4

INGREDIENTS

4½ tsp vegetable oil, plus extra
    for deep-frying
200 g/7 oz rice vermicelli noodles
1 onion, finely chopped
4 garlic cloves, finely chopped
1 boneless, skinless chicken
    breast, finely chopped

2 fresh red bird-eye chillies,
    deseeded and sliced
4 tbsp dried black mushrooms,
    soaked and thinly sliced
3 tbsp dried prawns
4 spring onions, sliced
3 tbsp lime juice
2 tbsp soy sauce

2 tbsp Thai fish sauce
2 tbsp rice vinegar
2 tbsp soft light brown sugar
2 eggs, beaten
3 tbsp chopped fresh coriander
spring onion curls, to garnish

1 Heat the vegetable oil for deep-frying in a large frying pan or wok until very hot. Add the noodles and deep-fry quickly, occasionally turning them, until puffed up, crisp and pale golden brown. Lift on to kitchen paper and drain well.

2 Heat 1 tablespoon of the oil and fry the onion and garlic for 1 minute. Add the chicken and stir-fry for 3 minutes. Add the chillies, mushrooms, dried prawns and spring onions.

3 Mix together the lime juice, soy sauce, fish sauce, rice vinegar and sugar, then stir into the pan and cook for a further minute. Remove the pan from the heat.

4 Heat the remaining oil in a wide pan and pour in the eggs to coat the base of the pan evenly, making a thin omelette. Cook until set and golden, then turn it over and cook the other side. Turn out and roll up, then slice into long ribbon strips.

5 Toss together the fried noodles, stir-fried ingredients, coriander and omelette strips. Garnish with spring onion curls and serve at once.

Sesame Noodles with Prawns & Coriander

Serves 4

INGREDIENTS

1 garlic clove, chopped	1 handful fresh coriander	2 tbsp lime juice
1 spring onion, chopped	300 g/10½ oz fine egg noodles	2 tbsp Thai fish sauce
1 small fresh red chilli, deseeded and sliced	2 tbsp vegetable oil	1 tsp sesame seeds, toasted
	2 tsp sesame oil	
	1 tsp shrimp paste	
	225 g/8 oz raw prawns, peeled	

1 Place the garlic, onion, chilli and coriander into mortar and grind with a pestle to a smooth paste.

2 Drop the egg noodles into a pan of boiling water and bring back to the boil, then simmer gently for 4 minutes or according to the packet instructions.

3 Meanwhile, heat the vegetable and sesame oils in a pan and stir in the shrimp paste and ground coriander mixture. Stir over a medium heat for 1 minute.

4 Stir in the prawns and stir-fry for 2 minutes until they have changed colour. Stir in the lime juice and fish sauce and cook for a further minute.

5 Drain the noodles and toss them into the wok. Sprinkle with the sesame seeds and serve.

COOK'S TIP

The roots of coriander are widely used in Thai cooking, so if you can buy fresh coriander with the root attached, the whole plant can be used in this dish for maximum flavour. If not, just use the stems and leaves.

Hot & Sour Noodles

Serves 4

INGREDIENTS

250 g/9 oz dried medium
  egg noodles
1 tbsp sesame oil
1 tbsp chilli oil
1 garlic clove, crushed
2 spring onions, finely chopped

55 g/2 oz button
  mushrooms, sliced
40 g/1½ oz dried Chinese black
  mushrooms, soaked, drained
  and sliced
2 tbsp lime juice
3 tbsp light soy sauce
1 tsp sugar

TO SERVE
shredded Chinese leaves
2 tbsp shredded coriander
2 tbsp chopped toasted peanuts

1 Cook the noodles in a large pan of boiling water for 3–4 minutes or according to the packet instructions. Drain well, return to the pan, toss with the sesame oil and set aside.

2 Heat the chilli oil in a large frying pan or wok and quickly stir-fry the garlic, onions and sliced button mushrooms to soften them.

3 Add the black mushrooms, lime juice, soy sauce and sugar and continue stir-frying until the mixture boiling. Add the noodles and toss to mix.

4 Serve immediately spooned over Chinese leaves, sprinkled with coriander and peanuts.

COOK'S TIP

Thai chilli oil is very hot, so if you want a milder flavour, use vegetable oil for the initial cooking instead, then add a final dribble of chilli oil just for seasoning.

Pad Thai Noodles

Serves 4

INGREDIENTS

250 g/9 oz rice stick noodles
3 tbsp groundnut oil
3 garlic cloves, finely chopped
125 g/4½ oz pork fillet, chopped
into 5 mm/¼ inch pieces
200 g/7 oz peeled cooked prawns
1 tbsp sugar
3 tbsp Thai fish sauce

1 tbsp tomato ketchup
1 tbsp lime juice
2 eggs, beaten
125 g/4½ oz beansprouts

TO GARNISH
1 tsp dried red chilli flakes
2 spring onions, thickly sliced
2 tbsp chopped fresh coriander

1 Soak the rice noodles in hot water for about 15 minutes, or according to the packet instructions. Drain thoroughly and put to one side.

2 Heat the oil in a large frying pan or wok and fry the garlic over a high heat for 30 seconds. Add the pork and stir-fry for 2–3 minutes until browned all over.

3 Stir in the prawns, then add the sugar, fish sauce, ketchup and lime juice and continue stir-frying for a further 30 seconds.

4 Stir in the eggs and stir-fry until lightly set. Stir in the noodles, then add the beansprouts and stir-fry for a further 30 seconds to cook lightly.

5 Turn out on to a serving dish and scatter with chilli flakes, spring onions and chopped coriander. Serve immediately.

COOK'S TIP

Drain the rice noodles before adding to the pan, as excess moisture will spoil the texture of the dish.

Rice Noodles with Mushrooms & Tofu

Serves 4

INGREDIENTS

225 g/8 oz rice stick noodles
2 tbsp vegetable oil
1 garlic clove, finely chopped
2 cm/¾ inch piece fresh root
    ginger, finely chopped
4 shallots, thinly sliced

70 g/2½ oz shiitake
    mushrooms, sliced
100 g/3½ oz firm tofu, cut into
    1.5 cm/⅝ inch dice
2 tbsp light soy sauce
1 tbsp rice wine

1 tbsp Thai fish sauce
1 tbsp smooth peanut butter
1 tsp chilli sauce
2 tbsp chopped toasted peanuts
shredded basil leaves, to garnish

1 Soak the rice stick noodles in hot water for 15 minutes or according to the packet instructions. Drain well.

2 Heat the vegetable oil in a pan and stir-fry the garlic, ginger and shallots for 1–2 minutes until softened and lightly browned.

3 Add the mushrooms and stir-fry for a further 2–3 minutes. Stir in the tofu and toss gently until lightly golden brown.

4 Mix together the soy sauce, rice wine, fish sauce, peanut butter and fish sauce, then stir into the pan.

5 Stir in the rice noodles and toss to coat evenly in the sauce. Scatter with peanuts and shredded basil leaves and serve hot.

COOK'S TIP

For an easy store-cupboard dish, replace the shiitake mushrooms with a can of Chinese straw mushrooms. Alternatively, use dried shiitake mushrooms, soaked and drained before use.

Thai-style Noodle Rostis

Serves 4

INGREDIENTS

125 g/4½ oz vermicelli
    rice noodles
2 spring onions, finely shredded
1 lemon grass stalk,
    finely shredded

3 tbsp fresh coconut,
    finely shredded
salt and pepper
vegetable oil, for frying
whole red chillies, to garnish

TO SERVE
115 g/4 oz beansprouts
1 small red onion, thinly sliced
1 avocado, thinly sliced
2 tbsp lime juice
2 tbsp rice wine
1 tsp chilli sauce

1 Break the rice noodles into short pieces and soak in hot water for about 4 minutes or according to the packet instructions. Drain thoroughly and pat dry with kitchen paper.

2 Stir together the noodles, spring onions, lemon grass and coconut.

3 Heat a small amount of oil in a heavy-based frying pan until very hot. Brush a 9 cm/3½ inch round biscuit cutter with oil and place in the pan. Spoon a small amount of noodle mixture into the cutter just to cover the base of the pan, then press down lightly with the back of a spoon.

4 Fry for 30 seconds, then carefully remove the cutter and continue frying the rösti until it is golden brown, turning it over once with a fish slice or spatula. Remove and drain on kitchen paper. Repeat with the remaining noodles, to make about 12 röstis.

5 To serve, arrange the noodle röstis in small stacks, with beansprouts, onion and avocado between the layers. Mix the lime juice, rice wine and chilli sauce together and spoon over just before serving, garnished with red chillies.

Drunken Noodles

Serves 4

INGREDIENTS

175 g/6 oz rice stick noodles
2 tbsp vegetable oil
1 garlic clove, crushed
2 small fresh green
   chillies, chopped
1 small onion, thinly sliced

150 g/5½ oz lean minced pork
   or chicken
1 small green pepper, deseeded
   and finely chopped
4 kaffir lime leaves,
   finely shredded
1 tbsp dark soy sauce

1 tbsp light soy sauce
½ tsp sugar
1 tomato, cut into thin wedges
2 tbsp sweet basil leaves, finely
   sliced, to garnish

1 Soak the rice stick noodles in hot water for 15 minutes or according to the packet instructions. Drain well.

2 Heat the oil in a wok and stir-fry the garlic, chillies and onion for 1 minute.

3 Stir in the pork or chicken and stir-fry over a high heat for a further minute, then add the pepper and continue stir-frying for a further 2 minutes.

4 Stir in the lime leaves, dark and light soy sauces and sugar. Add the noodles and tomato and toss well to heat thoroughly.

5 Serve hot, sprinkled with the sliced basil leaves.

COOK'S TIP

Fresh kaffir lime leaves freeze well, so if you buy more than you need, simply tie them in a tightly sealed polythene freezer bag and freeze for up to a month. They can be used straight from the freezer.

Crispy Duck with Noodles & Tamarind

Serves 4

INGREDIENTS

3 duck breasts, total weight about 400 g/14 oz	½ tsp five-spice powder	100 g/3½ oz mangetouts
2 garlic cloves, crushed	250 g/9 oz rice stick noodles	2 tbsp tamarind juice
1½ tsp chilli paste	1 tsp vegetable oil	sesame seeds, to garnish
1 tbsp clear honey	1 tsp sesame oil	
3 tbsp dark soy sauce	2 spring onion, sliced	

1 Prick the duck breast skin all over with a fork and place in a deep dish.

2 Mix together the garlic, chilli, honey, soy sauce and five-spice powder, then pour over the duck. Turn the breasts over to coat them evenly, then cover and set aside to marinate in the refrigerator for at least 1 hour.

3 Meanwhile, soak the rice noodles in hot water for 15 minutes. Drain well.

4 Drain the duck breasts from the marinade and place on a grill rack. Cook under a preheated hot grill for about 10 minutes, turning them over occasionally, until they become a rich golden brown. Remove and slice the duck breasts thinly.

5 Heat the vegetable and sesame oils in a large, heavy-based frying pan and stir-fry the spring onions and mangetouts for 2 minutes. Stir in the reserved marinade and tamarind and bring the mixture to the boil.

6 Add the sliced duck and noodles and toss to heat through. Serve immediately, sprinkled with sesame seeds.

Rice Noodles with Chicken & Chinese Leaves

Serves 4

INGREDIENTS

200 g/7 oz rice stick noodles
1 tbsp sunflower oil
1 garlic clove, finely chopped
2 cm/³⁄₄ inch piece fresh root
    ginger, finely chopped
4 spring onions, chopped
1 fresh red bird-eye chilli,
    deseeded and sliced

300 g/10¹⁄₂ oz boneless, skinless
    chicken, finely chopped
2 chicken livers, finely chopped
1 celery stick, thinly sliced
1 carrot, cut into
    fine matchsticks
300 g/10¹⁄₂ oz shredded Chinese
    leaves
4 tbsp lime juice

2 tbsp Thai fish sauce
1 tbsp soy sauce

TO GARNISH
2 tbsp shredded fresh mint
slices of pickled garlic
fresh mint sprig

1 Cover the rice noodles with hot water and leave to soak for 15 minutes or according to the packet instructions. Drain well.

2 Heat the oil in a wok or large, heavy-based frying pan and stir-fry the garlic, ginger, spring onions and chilli for about 1 minute. Stir in the chicken and chicken livers, then stir-fry over a high heat for 2–3 minutes until beginning to brown.

3 Stir in the celery and carrot and stir-fry for 2 minutes to soften. Add the Chinese leaves, then stir in the lime juice, fish sauce and soy sauce.

4 Add the noodles and stir to heat thoroughly. Sprinkle with shredded mint and pickled garlic. Serve immediately, garnished with a mint sprig.

Rice Noodles with Spinach

Serves 4

INGREDIENTS

115 g/4 oz thin rice stick noodles
2 tbsp dried prawns (optional)

250 g/9 oz fresh young spinach
1 tbsp groundnut oil
2 garlic cloves, finely chopped
2 tsp Thai green curry paste

1 tsp sugar
1 tbsp light soy sauce

1 Soak the noodles in hot water for 15 minutes or according to the packet instructions, then drain well.

2 Soak the prawns in hot water for 10 minutes and drain well. Wash the spinach thoroughly, drain well and remove any tough stalks.

3 Heat the oil in a large, heavy-based frying pan or wok and stir-fry the garlic over a medium-low heat for 1 minute. Stir in the curry paste and stir-fry for 30 seconds. Stir in the soaked prawns and stir-fry for 30 seconds.

4 Add the spinach and stir-fry for 1–2 minutes until the leaves are just wilted.

5 Stir in the sugar and soy sauce, then add the noodles and toss thoroughly to mix evenly. Serve immediately while hot.

COOK'S TIP

It is best to choose young spinach leaves for this dish, as they are beautifully tender and cook within a matter of seconds. If you can only get older spinach, however, shred the leaves before adding to the dish so they cook more quickly.

Egg Noodle Salad with Coconut, Lime & Basil Dressing

Serves 4

INGREDIENTS

225 g/8 oz dried egg noodles
2 tsp sesame oil
1 carrot
100 g/3½ oz beansprouts
½ cucumber
150 g/5½ oz cooked turkey breast
    meat, shredded into
    thin slivers

2 spring onions, finely shredded

DRESSING
5 tbsp coconut milk
3 tbsp lime juice
1 tbsp light soy sauce
2 tsp Thai fish sauce
1 tsp chilli oil

1 tsp sugar
2 tbsp chopped fresh coriander
2 tbsp chopped fresh sweet basil

TO GARNISH
peanuts
chopped fresh basil leaves

1 Cook the noodles in boiling water for 4 minutes or according to the packet instructions. Plunge them into a bowl of cold water to cool, then drain and toss in sesame oil.

2 Use a vegetable peeler to shave off thin ribbons from the carrot. Blanch the ribbons and beansprouts in boiling water for 30 seconds, drain, then plunge into cold water for 30 seconds. Drain well again. Next, shave thin ribbons of cucumber with the peeler.

3 Toss the carrots, beansprouts, cucumber and spring onions together with the turkey and noodles.

4 Place the dressing ingredients in a screw-top jar and shake vigorously to mix evenly.

5 Add the dressing to the noodle mixture and toss. Pile on to a serving dish. Sprinkle with peanuts and basil. Serve cold.

Stir-fried Rice with Egg Strips

Serves 4

INGREDIENTS

2 tbsp groundnut oil
1 egg, beaten with 1 tsp water
1 garlic clove, finely chopped
1 small onion, finely chopped
1 tbsp Thai red curry paste
250 g/9 oz long-grain
    rice, cooked

55 g/2 oz cooked peas
1 tbsp Thai fish sauce
2 tbsp tomato ketchup
2 tbsp chopped fresh coriander

TO GARNISH
fresh red chillies
cucumber slices

1 To make chilli flowers, hold the stem with your fingertips and use a small sharp, pointed knife to cut a slit down the length from near the stem end to the tip. Turn the chilli about a quarter turn and make another cut. Repeat to make a total of 4 cuts, then scrape out the seeds. Cut each 'petal' again in half, or into quarters, to make 8–16 petals. Place the chilli in iced water.

2 Heat about 1 teaspoon of the oil in a wok. Pour in the egg mixture, swirling it to coat the pan evenly and make a thin layer. When set and golden, remove the egg from the pan and roll up. Keep to one side.

3 Add the remaining groundnut oil to the pan and stir-fry the garlic and onion over a medium heat for 1 minute. Add the red curry paste and stir in the cooked rice and peas.

4 Stir in the fish sauce and ketchup. Remove the pan from the heat and pile the rice on to a serving dish.

5 Slice the egg roll into spiral strips, without unrolling, and use to garnish the rice. Add the cucumber slices and chilli flowers. Serve hot.

Jasmine Rice with Lemon & Basil

Serves 4

INGREDIENTS

400 g/14 oz jasmine rice
800 ml/28 fl oz water
rind of ½ lemon, finely grated
2 tbsp chopped fresh sweet basil

1 Wash the rice in several changes of cold water until the water runs clear. Bring the water to the boil in a large pan, then add the rice.

2 Bring back to a rolling boil. Turn the heat to a low simmer, cover the pan and simmer for a further 12 minutes.

3 Remove the pan from the heat and leave to stand, covered, for 10 minutes.

4 Fluff up the rice with a fork, then stir in the lemon rind. Serve scattered with basil.

COOK'S TIP

It is important to leave the pan tightly covered while the rice cooks and steams inside so the grains cook evenly and become fluffy and separate.

Rice with Seafood

Serves 4

INGREDIENTS

12 live mussels, cleaned
2 litres/3½ pints fish stock
2 tbsp vegetable oil
1 garlic clove, crushed
1 tsp grated fresh root ginger
1 fresh red bird-eye
    chilli, chopped

2 spring onions, chopped
225 g/8 oz long grain rice
2 small squid, cleaned and sliced
100 g/3½ oz firm white fish fillet,
    such as halibut or monkfish,
    cut into chunks

100 g/3½ oz raw prawns, peeled
2 tbsp Thai fish sauce
3 tbsp shredded fresh coriander

1 Discard any mussels with damaged shells or open ones that do not close when firmly tapped on a work surface. Heat 4 tablespoons of the stock in a large pan. Add the mussels, cover and shake the pan over a medium heat until the mussels open. Remove the pan from the heat and discard any mussels which do not open.

2 Heat the oil in a large frying pan or wok and fry the garlic, ginger, chilli and spring onions for 30 seconds. Add the stock and bring to the boil.

3 Stir in the rice, then add the squid, fish fillet and prawns. Lower the heat and simmer for 15 minutes, or until the rice is cooked. Add the fish sauce and mussels.

4 Ladle into wide bowls and sprinkle with coriander, before serving.

COOK'S TIP

You could use leftover cooked rice for this dish. Just simmer the seafood gently until cooked, then stir in the rice at the end.

Coconut Rice with Pineapple

Serves 4

INGREDIENTS

200 g/7 oz long-grain rice
500 ml/18 fl oz coconut milk

2 lemon grass stalks
200 ml/7 fl oz water
2 slices fresh pineapple, peeled
and diced

2 tbsp toasted coconut
chilli sauce, to serve

1 Wash the rice in several changes of cold water until the water runs clear. Place in a large pan with the coconut milk.

2 Place the lemon grass on a firm work surface and bruise it by hitting firmly with a rolling pin or meat mallet. Add to the pan with the rice and coconut milk.

3 Add the water and bring to the boil. Lower the heat, cover the pan tightly and simmer gently for 15 minutes. Remove the pan from the heat and fluff up the rice with a fork.

4 Remove the lemon grass and stir in the pineapple. Scatter with toasted coconut and serve with chilli sauce.

VARIATION

A sweet version of this dish can be made by simply omitting the lemon grass and stirring in palm sugar or caster sugar to taste during cooking. Serve as a dessert, with extra pineapple slices.

Vegetables *Salads*

Many of the local vegetables, salad leaves and shoots
which Thais use in vegetable dishes and salads are
native, often growing wild locally and are uncultivated.
This makes it difficult to produce really authentic Thai
salads at home, as even the best Oriental food stores can
not source all the fresh ingredients.

You may be reduced to substituting a few fresh
ingredients with canned ones, or local Thai vegetables
with more familiar Western ones, but luckily you can
now buy a good selection of cultivated Oriental
vegetables such as pak choi and Chinese leaves.
So, with a few careful choices, it's easy to produce
some imaginative vegetable dishes with distinctly
Thai flavours.

A Thai salad can make a stunning centrepiece for any
dinner table. Thai cooks usually add strips of finely
chopped cooked meat, fish or shellfish to their salads, or
for vegetarian dishes, mushrooms or tofu will appear.

Dressings are typically piquant and spicy, with the usual
skillful balance of bitter, salt, sour, hot and sweet tastes.
To finish, a sprinkling of crushed peanuts or dried
chillies, chopped coriander or mint, slices of pickled
garlic, and a final flourish of chilli flowers or spring
onion tassels will add colour to the dish.

Crisp Pickled Vegetables

Serves 6–8

INGREDIENTS

½ small cauliflower	500 ml/18 fl oz rice vinegar	3 fresh red bird-eye chillies
½ cucumber	1 tbsp caster sugar	5 tbsp groundnut oil
2 carrots	1 tsp salt	
200 g/7 oz French beans	3 garlic cloves	
½ small Chinese cabbage	3 shallots	

1 Trim the cauliflower. Peel and deseed the cucumber. Peel the carrots. Top and tail the beans. Trim the cabbage, then cut all the vegetables into bite-size pieces. If you have time, cut the carrots into flower shapes.

2 Place the rice vinegar, sugar and salt in a large pan and bring almost to the boil. Add the vegetables, lower the heat and simmer for 3–4 minutes until they are just tender, but still crisp inside. Remove the pan from the heat and leave the vegetables to cool in the liquid in the pan.

3 Peel the garlic and shallots and deseed the chillies. Place in a mortar and grind with a pestle until a smooth paste forms.

4 Heat the oil in a frying pan and stir-fry the spice paste gently for 1–2 minutes. Add the vegetables with the vinegar and cook for a further 2 minutes to reduce the liquid slightly. Remove from the heat and set aside to cool completely.

5 Serve the pickles cold, or pack into jars and store in the refrigerator for up to 2 weeks.

COOK'S TIP

To make simple carrot flowers, peel the carrot thinly as usual, then use a canelle knife or small sharp knife to cut narrow 'channels' down the length of it at regular intervals. Slice the carrot as usual and the slices will resemble flowers.

Chilli & Coconut Sambal

Serves 6–8

INGREDIENTS

1 small coconut
1 slice fresh pineapple, finely diced
1 small onion, finely chopped

2 small fresh green chillies, deseeded and chopped
5 cm/2 inch piece lemon grass
½ tsp salt
1 tsp shrimp paste

1 tbsp lime juice
2 tbsp fresh coriander, chopped
fresh coriander sprigs, to garnish

1 Puncture 2 of the coconut eyes with a screwdriver and pour the milk out from the shell. Crack the coconut shell, prise away the flesh and coarsely grate it into a bowl.

2 Mix the coconut with the pineapple, onion, chillies and lemon grass.

3 Blend together the salt, shrimp paste and lime juice, then stir into the prepared sambal.

4 Stir in the coriander. Spoon into a small dish to serve and garnish with fresh coriander sprigs.

COOK'S TIP

The coconut can be grated quickly by using a grating blade on a food processor.

VARIATION

To make a quicker version of this sambal, stir a teaspoon of Thai green curry paste into freshly grated coconut and add finely diced pineapple and lime juice to taste.

Mixed Vegetables in Peanut Sauce

Serves 4

INGREDIENTS

2 carrots
1 small cauliflower
2 small heads green pak choi
150 g/5½ oz French beans,
   topped and tailed, if wished

2 tbsp vegetable oil
1 garlic clove, finely chopped
6 spring onions, sliced
1 tsp chilli paste
2 tbsp soy sauce

2 tbsp rice wine
4 tbsp smooth peanut butter
3 tbsp coconut milk

1 First, prepare the vegetables. Cut the carrots diagonally into thin slices. Cut the cauliflower into small florets, then slice the stalk thinly. Thickly slice the pak choi. Finally, chop the French beans into 3 cm/1¼ inch lengths.

2 Heat the oil in a large frying pan or wok and stir-fry the garlic and spring onions for about 1 minute. Stir in the chilli paste and cook for a few seconds.

3 Add the carrots and cauliflower and stir-fry for 2–3 minutes.

4 Add the pak choi and beans and stir-fry for a further 2 minutes. Stir in the soy sauce and rice wine.

5 Mix the peanut butter with the coconut milk and stir into the pan, then cook, stirring, for a further minute. Serve immediately while still hot.

COOK'S TIP

It's important to cut the vegetables thinly into even-size pieces so they cook quickly and evenly. Prepare all the vegetables before you start to cook.

Thai Red Bean Curry

Serves 4

INGREDIENTS

400 g/14 oz French beans
1 garlic clove, finely sliced
1 fresh red bird-eye chilli, deseeded and chopped
½ tsp paprika pepper

1 piece lemon grass stalk, finely chopped
2 tsp Thai fish sauce
125 ml/4 fl oz coconut milk

1 tbsp sunflower oil
2 spring onions, sliced

1 Cut the French beans into 5 cm/2 inch pieces and cook in boiling water for about 2 minutes. Drain well.

2 Place the garlic, chilli, paprika, lemon grass, fish sauce and coconut milk in a blender and process until a smooth paste forms.

3 Heat the sunflower oil in a wok or large, heavy-based frying pan. Add the spring onions and stir-fry over a high heat for about 1 minute. Stir in the spice paste and bring the mixture to the boil.

4 Lower the heat and simmer for 3–4 minutes to reduce the liquid by about half. Add the beans and simmer for a further 1–2 minutes until tender. Serve hot.

COOK'S TIP

Young runner beans can be used instead of French beans. Remove any strings from the beans, then cut at a diagonal angle in short lengths. Cook as the recipe until tender.

Stir-fried Ginger Mushrooms

Serves 4

INGREDIENTS

2 tbsp vegetable oil
3 garlic cloves, crushed
1 tbsp Thai red curry paste
½ tsp ground turmeric
425 g/15 oz can Chinese straw
   mushrooms, drained, rinsed
   and halved
2 cm/¾ inch piece fresh root
   ginger, finely shredded
100 ml/3½ fl oz coconut milk

40 g/1½ oz dried Chinese black
   mushrooms, soaked, drained
   and sliced
1 tbsp lemon juice
1 tbsp light soy sauce
2 tsp sugar
8 cherry tomatoes, halved
200 g/7oz firm tofu, diced
½ tsp salt

fresh coriander leaves, to garnish
boiled fragrant rice, to serve

1 Heat the oil and fry the garlic for about 1 minute, stirring. Stir in the curry paste and turmeric and cook for about a further 30 seconds.

2 Stir in the straw mushrooms and ginger and stir-fry for 2 minutes. Stir in the coconut milk and bring to the boil.

3 Stir in the Chinese dried black mushrooms, lemon juice, soy sauce, sugar and salt and heat thoroughly. Add the tomatoes and tofu and toss gently to heat through.

4 Scatter the coriander leaves over the mixture and serve immediately, with fragrant rice.

COOK'S TIP

You can vary the mushrooms depending on your own taste – try a mixture of oyster and shiitake for a change – or even just ordinary cultivated button mushrooms are very tasty cooked this way.

Thai-spiced Mushrooms

Serves 4

INGREDIENTS

8 large, flat mushrooms
3 tbsp sunflower oil
2 tbsp light soy sauce
1 garlic clove, crushed
2 cm/¾ inch piece fresh galangal
    or fresh root ginger, grated

1 tbsp Thai green curry paste
8 baby sweetcorn cobs, sliced
3 spring onions, chopped
125 g/4½ oz beansprouts
100 g/3½ oz firm tofu, diced
2 tsp sesame seeds, toasted,

TO SERVE
chopped cucumber
sliced red pepper

1 Remove the stalks from the mushrooms and set aside. Place the caps on a baking tray. Combine 2 tablespoons of the oil with 1 tablespoon of the light soy sauce and brush the mixture over the mushroom caps.

2 Grill the mushroom caps under a preheated hot grill until golden and tender, turning them over once.

3 Meanwhile, chop the mushroom stalks finely. Heat the remaining oil in a wok or large frying pan and stir-fry the stalks with the garlic and galangal or ginger for 1 minute.

4 Stir in the curry paste and add the baby sweetcorn cobs and spring onions. Stir-fry for 1 minute. Add the beansprouts and stir-fry for a further minute.

5 Add the tofu and the remaining soy sauce, then toss lightly until heated through. Remove the wok or pan from the heat and spoon the vegetable mixture into the mushroom caps.

6 Sprinkle with the sesame seeds. Serve immediately with chopped cucumber and sliced red pepper.

COOK'S TIP

Galangal or ginger can be frozen for several weeks, either peeled and finely chopped ready to add to dishes, or in whole pieces. Defrost the piece or grate finely from frozen.

Oriental Vegetables with Yellow Bean Sauce

Serves 4

INGREDIENTS

1 aubergine
2 tbsp vegetable oil
3 garlic cloves, crushed
4 spring onions, chopped
1 small red pepper, deseeded and
    thinly sliced
4 baby sweetcorn cobs, halved
    lengthways
85 g/3 oz mangetouts

200 g/7 oz Chinese mustard
    greens, coarsely shredded
425 g/15 oz can Chinese straw
    mushrooms, drained
    and rinsed
125 g/4½ oz/ beansprouts
2 tbsp rice wine
2 tbsp yellow bean sauce
2 tbsp dark soy sauce

1 tsp chilli sauce
1 tsp sugar
125 ml/4 fl oz chicken or
    vegetable stock
1 tsp cornflour
2 tsp water
salt

1 Trim the aubergine and cut into 5 cm/2 inch long matchsticks. Place in a colander, sprinkle with salt and leave to drain for about 30 minutes. Rinse in cold water and pat dry with kitchen paper.

2 Heat the oil in a large frying pan or wok and stir-fry the garlic, spring onions and red pepper over a high heat for 1 minute. Stir in the aubergine pieces and stir-fry for a further minute or until softened.

3 Stir in the sweetcorn and mangetouts and stir-fry for about 1 minute. Then add the mustard greens, mushrooms and beansprouts and stir-fry for 30 seconds.

4 Mix together the rice wine, yellow bean sauce, soy sauce, chilli sauce and sugar and add to the pan with the stock. Bring to the boil, stirring.

5 Blend the cornflour with the water to form a smooth paste. Stir quickly into the pan or wok and cook for a further minute. Serve immediately.

Potatoes in Creamed Coconut

Serves 4

INGREDIENTS

600 g/1 lb 5 oz potatoes	½ tsp salt	350 ml/12 fl oz vegetable or
1 onion, thinly sliced	½ tsp pepper	chicken stock
2 fresh red bird-eye chillies,	85 g/3 oz creamed coconut	chopped fresh coriander or basil,
finely chopped		to garnish

1 Peel the potatoes thinly. Use a sharp knife to cut into 2 cm/¾ inch chunks.

2 Place the potatoes in a pan with the onion, chillies, salt, pepper and creamed coconut. Stir in the stock.

3 Bring to the boil, stirring, then lower the heat, cover and simmer gently, stirring occasionally, until the potatoes are tender.

4 Adjust the seasoning to taste, then sprinkle with chopped coriander or basil. Serve the potatoes immediately while hot.

COOK'S TIP

If the potatoes are a thin-skinned, or a new variety, simply wash or scrub to remove any dirt and cook with the skins on. This adds extra dietary fibre and nutrients to the finished dish, and cuts down on the preparation time. Baby new potatoes can be cooked whole.

Stir-fried Broccoli in Oyster Sauce

Serves 4

INGREDIENTS

400 g/14 oz broccoli
1 tbsp groundnut oil
2 shallots, finely chopped

1 garlic clove, finely chopped
1 tbsp rice wine or sherry
5 tbsp oyster sauce

¼ tsp ground black pepper
1 tsp chilli oil

1 Trim the broccoli and cut into small florets. Blanch in a pan of boiling water for about 30 seconds, then drain well.

2 Heat the oil in a large frying pan or wok and stir-fry the shallots and garlic for 1–2 minutes until they are golden brown.

3 Tip in the broccoli and stir-fry for 2 minutes. Add the rice wine and oyster sauce and then stir for a further minute.

4 Stir in the pepper and drizzle with a little chilli oil just before serving.

COOK'S TIP

To make chilli oil, tuck fresh red or green chillies into a jar and top up with olive oil or a light vegetable oil. Cover with a lid and leave to infuse the flavour for at least 3 weeks before using.

Roasted Thai-spiced Peppers

Serves 4

INGREDIENTS

2 red peppers
2 yellow peppers
2 green peppers
2 fresh red bird-eye chillies,
    deseeded and finely chopped

1 lemon grass stalk,
    finely shredded
4 tbsp lime juice
2 tbsp palm sugar
1 tbsp Thai fish sauce

1 Roast the peppers under a preheated hot grill, barbecue over hot coals or roast in a hot oven, turning them over occasionally, until the skins are charred. Cool slightly, then remove the skins. Cut each pepper in half and remove and discard the core and seeds.

2 Slice the peppers thickly and transfer to a large mixing bowl.

3 Place the chillies, lemon grass, lime juice, sugar and fish sauce in a screw-top jar and shake well until thoroughly mixed.

4 Pour the dressing evenly over the peppers and toss to coat. Allow to cool completely, cover with clingfilm and chill in the refrigerator for at least an hour before serving. Transfer to a serving dish to serve.

COOK'S TIP

The flavours will mingle best if the peppers are still slightly warm when you spoon the dressing over them. Prepare the dressing while the peppers are cooking, so it's ready to pour over when they are cooked.

Pak Choi with Crab Meat

Serves 4

INGREDIENTS

2 heads green pak choi, about
  250 g/9 oz total weight
2 tbsp vegetable oil
1 garlic clove, thinly sliced

2 tbsp oyster sauce
100 g/3½ oz cherry
  tomatoes, halved

170 g/6 oz can white crab
  meat, drained
salt and pepper

1 Trim the pak choi and cut into 2.5 cm/1 inch thick slices.

2 Heat the oil in a large, heavy-based frying pan or wok and stir-fry the garlic quickly over a high heat for 1 minute.

3 Add the pak choi and stir-fry for 2–3 minutes until the leaves wilt, but the stalks are still crisp.

4 Add the oyster sauce and tomatoes and stir-fry for a further minute.

5 Add the crab meat and season well with salt and pepper. Stir well to heat thoroughly and break up the distribution of crab meat before serving.

VARIATION

For a vegetarian version of this dish, omit the crab meat and replace the oyster sauce with 2 tablespoons of light soy sauce.

If pak choi is not available, Chinese leaves make a good alternative for this dish.

Spiced Cashew Nut Curry

Serves 4

INGREDIENTS

250 g/9 oz unsalted cashew nuts
1 tsp coriander seeds
1 tsp cumin seeds
2 cardamom pods, crushed
1 tbsp sunflower oil
1 onion, thinly sliced
1 garlic clove, crushed

1 small fresh green chilli,
    deseeded and chopped
1 cinnamon stick
½ tsp ground turmeric
4 tbsp coconut cream

300 ml/10 fl oz hot
    vegetable stock
3 kaffir lime leaves,
    finely shredded
salt and pepper
boiled jasmine rice, to serve

1 Soak the cashew nuts in cold water overnight. Drain thoroughly. Crush the coriander, cumin seeds and cardamom pods in a mortar with a pestle.

2 Heat the oil and stir-fry the onion and garlic for 2–3 minutes to soften, but not brown. Add the chilli, crushed spices, cinnamon stick and turmeric and stir-fry for a further minute.

3 Add the coconut cream and the hot stock to the pan. Bring to the boil, then add the cashew nuts and lime leaves.

4 Cover the pan, lower the heat and simmer gently for about 20 minutes. Serve hot, accompanied by jasmine rice.

COOK'S TIP

All spices give the best flavour when freshly crushed, but if you prefer, you can use ground spices instead of crushing them yourself with a pestle and mortar.

Potato & Spinach Yellow Curry

Serves 4

INGREDIENTS

2 garlic cloves, finely chopped
3 cm/1¼ inch piece galangal,
　finely chopped
1 lemon grass stalk,
　finely chopped
1 tsp coriander seeds
3 tbsp vegetable oil

2 tsp Thai red curry paste
½ tsp ground turmeric
200 ml/7 fl oz coconut milk
250 g/9 oz potatoes, peeled and
　cut into 2 cm/¾ inch cubes

100 ml/3½ fl oz vegetable stock
200 g/7 oz young spinach leaves
1 small onion, thinly sliced
　into rings

1 Place the garlic, galangal, lemon grass and coriander seeds in a mortar and pound with a pestle until a smooth paste forms.

2 Heat 2 tablespoons of the vegetable oil in a frying pan or wok. Stir in the paste and stir-fry for about 30 seconds. Stir in the curry paste and turmeric, then add the coconut milk and bring to the boil.

3 Add the potatoes and stock. Return to the boil, then lower the heat and simmer, uncovered, for 10–12 minutes until the potatoes are almost tender.

4 Stir in the spinach and simmer until the leaves are wilted.

5 Meanwhile, fry the onion in the remaining oil until crisp and golden brown. Place on top of the curry just before serving.

COOK'S TIP

Choose a firm, waxy potato for this dish, one that will keep its shape during cooking in preference to a floury variety which will break up easily once cooked.

Sweet Potato Cakes with Soy-tomato Sauce

Serves 4

INGREDIENTS

2 sweet potatoes, 500 g/1 lb 2 oz
    total weight
2 garlic cloves, crushed
1 small fresh green
    chilli, chopped
2 coriander sprigs, chopped

1 tbsp dark soy sauce
plain flour, for shaping
vegetable oil, for frying
sesame seeds, for sprinkling

SOY-TOMATO SAUCE
2 tsp vegetable oil
1 garlic clove, finely chopped
2 cm/¾ inch piece fresh root
    ginger, finely chopped
3 tomatoes, peeled and chopped
2 tbsp dark soy sauce
1 tbsp lime juice
2 tbsp chopped fresh coriander

1 Make the soy-tomato sauce. Heat the oil in a wok and stir-fry the garlic and ginger for about 1 minute. Add the tomatoes and stir-fry for a further 2 minutes. Remove from the heat and stir in the soy sauce, lime and coriander. Set aside and keep warm.

2 Peel the sweet potatoes and grate finely (you can do this quickly with a food processor). Place the garlic, chilli and coriander in a mortar and crush with a pestle to a smooth paste. Stir in the soy sauce and then mix with the sweet potatoes.

3 Divide the mixture into 12 equal portions. Dip each piece into flour and pat into a flat, round patty shape between your palms.

4 Heat a shallow layer of oil in a wide frying pan. Fry the sweet potato patties over a high heat until golden, turning once.

5 Drain on kitchen paper and sprinkle with sesame seeds. Serve hot, with a spoonful of the soy-tomato sauce.

Thai-style Sweetcorn Fritters

Serves 4

INGREDIENTS

55 g/2 oz plain flour
1 large egg
2 tsp Thai green curry paste
5 tbsp coconut milk
400 g/14 oz canned or frozen
    sweetcorn kernels
4 spring onions
1 tbsp chopped fresh coriander

1 tbsp chopped fresh basil
salt and pepper
vegetable oil, for frying

TO SERVE
lime wedges
chilli relish

1 Place the flour, egg, curry paste, coconut milk and about half the sweetcorn kernels in a food processor and process until a smooth, thick batter forms.

2 Finely chop the spring onions and stir into the batter with the remaining sweetcorn, chopped coriander and basil. Season well with salt and pepper.

3 Heat a small amount of oil in a wide, heavy-based frying pan. Drop in tablespoonfuls of the batter and cook for 2–3 minutes until golden brown.

4 Turn them over and cook for a further 2–3 minutes until golden. Fry in batches, making about 12–16 fritters in total, keeping the cooked fritters hot while you cook the remaining batter.

5 Serve the fritters hot, with lime wedges and a chilli relish.

COOK'S TIP

If you prefer to use fresh sweetcorn, strip the kernels from the cobs with a sharp knife, then cook in boiling water for about 4–5 minutes until just tender. Drain well before using as instructed.

Spicy Vegetable Fritters with Sweet Chilli Dip

Serves 4–6

INGREDIENTS

150 g/5½ oz plain flour
1 tsp ground coriander
1 tsp ground cumin
1 tsp ground turmeric
1 tsp salt
½ tsp pepper
2 garlic cloves, finely chopped
3 cm/1¼ inch piece fresh root
   ginger, chopped
2 small fresh green chillies,
   finely chopped

1 tbsp chopped fresh coriander
about 225 ml/8 fl oz water
1 onion, chopped
1 potato, coarsely grated
85 g/3 oz sweetcorn kernels
1 small aubergine, diced
125 g/4½ oz Chinese broccoli, cut
   into short lengths
coconut oil, for deep frying

SWEET CHILLI DIP
2 fresh red bird-eye chillies,
   finely chopped
4 tbsp caster sugar
4 tbsp rice vinegar
1 tbsp light soy sauce

1 Make the dip by mixing together all the ingredients, stirring well until the sugar is dissolved. Cover and set aside until it is needed.

2 For the fritters, place the flour in a bowl and stir in the ground coriander, cumin, turmeric, salt and pepper. Add the garlic, ginger, chillies and chopped coriander and then stir in just enough cold water to make a thick batter.

3 Add the onion, potato, sweetcorn, aubergine and broccoli to the batter and stir well to distribute the ingredients evenly.

4 Heat the oil in a wok to 190°C/375°F or until a cube of bread browns in 30 seconds. Drop tablespoons of the batter into the hot oil and fry, in batches, until golden and crisp, turning once.

5 Keep the first batches of fried fritters hot in a warm oven while you are cooking the others. Drain well on kitchen paper and serve at once while still hot, accompanied by the sweet chilli dip.

Aubergine- & Mushroom-stuffed Omelette

Serves 1–2

INGREDIENTS

3 tbsp vegetable oil
1 garlic clove, finely chopped
1 small onion, finely chopped
1 small aubergine, diced
½ small green pepper, deseeded and chopped

1 large dried Chinese black mushroom, soaked, drained and sliced
1 tomato, diced
1 tbsp light soy sauce
½ tsp sugar

¼ tsp pepper
2 large eggs
salad leaves, tomato wedges and cucumber slices, to garnish

1 Heat half the oil in a wok or large frying pan and fry the garlic over a high heat for 30 seconds. Add the onion and the aubergine and continue to stir-fry until golden.

2 Add the green pepper and stir-fry for a further minute to soften. Stir in the Chinese mushroom, tomato, soy sauce, sugar and pepper. Remove the vegetables from the pan and keep hot.

3 Beat the eggs together lightly. Heat the remaining oil, swirling to coat the wok or frying pan. Pour in the egg and swirl to set around the pan.

4 When the egg is set, spoon the filling into the centre. Fold in the sides of the omelette to make a square parcel.

5 Slide the omelette carefully on to a warmed dish and garnish with salad leaves, tomato wedges and cucumber slices. Serve hot.

COOK'S TIP

If you heat the pan thoroughly before adding the oil, and heat the oil before adding the ingredients, you should not have a problem with ingredients sticking to the pan.

Crispy Tofu with Chilli-soy Sauce

Serves 4

INGREDIENTS

300 g/10½ oz firm tofu
2 tbsp vegetable oil
1 garlic clove, sliced
1 carrot, cut into matchsticks

½ green pepper, deseeded and
   cut into matchsticks
1 fresh red bird-eye chilli,
   deseeded and finely chopped
2 tbsp soy sauce

1 tbsp lime juice
1 tbsp Thai fish sauce
1 tbsp soft light brown sugar
pickled garlic slices, to
   serve (optional)

1 Drain the tofu and pat dry with kitchen paper. Cut into 2 cm/¾ inch cubes.

2 Heat the oil in a wok and stir-fry the garlic for 1 minute. Remove the garlic and add the tofu, then fry quickly until well-browned, turning gently to brown on all sides.

3 Lift out the tofu, drain well and keep hot. Stir the carrot and pepper into the pan and stir-fry for 1 minute.

4 Spoon the carrot and peppers on to a dish and pile the tofu on top.

5 Mix together the chilli, soy sauce, lime juice, fish sauce and sugar, stirring until the sugar is dissolved.

6 Spoon the sauce over the tofu and serve topped with slices of pickled garlic, if you like. Serve hot.

COOK'S TIP

Make sure to buy firm fresh tofu for this dish – the softer 'silken' type is more like junket in texture and not firm enough to hold its shape well during frying. It is better for adding to soups.

Cucumber Salad

Serves 4

INGREDIENTS

1 cucumber
1 small red onion
1 garlic clove, crushed

½ tsp chilli paste
2 tsp Thai fish sauce
1 tbsp lime juice

1 tsp sesame oil
salt

1 Trim the cucumber and coarsely grate the flesh, without peeling. Place in a sieve over a bowl, sprinkle with 1 teaspoon salt and set aside to drain for 20 minutes. Discard the liquid.

2 Peel the onion and chop finely, then toss into the cucumber. Spoon the mixture into 4 individual bowls or 1 large one.

3 Mix together the garlic, chilli paste, fish sauce, lime juice and sesame oil, then spoon over the salad. Cover the salad and chill before serving.

COOK'S TIP

Once the salad is made, it can be chilled with the dressing for 1–2 hours, but is best eaten on the day of making.

VARIATION

For a change, peel the cucumber and cut it into small dice, then salt and drain as above. Drain and toss with the onions and dressing as before.

Thai Green Salad

Serves 4–6

INGREDIENTS

1 small head Cos lettuce
1 bunch spring onions
½ cucumber
4 tbsp fresh coconut, coarsely
    shredded and toasted

DRESSING
4 tbsp lime juice
2 tbsp Thai fish sauce
1 small fresh red bird-eye chilli,
    finely chopped
1 tsp sugar

1 garlic clove, crushed
2 tbsp chopped fresh coriander
1 tbsp chopped fresh mint

1 Tear or roughly shred the lettuce leaves and place in a large salad bowl.

2 Trim and thinly slice the spring onions at a diagonal angle, then add them to the salad bowl.

3 Use a vegetable peeler to shave thin slices along the length of the cucumber and add to the salad bowl.

4 Place all the ingredients for the dressing in a screw-top jar, close the lid tightly and shake vigorously to mix thoroughly.

5 Pour the dressing over the salad and toss well to coat the leaves evenly.

6 Scatter the coconut over the salad and toss in lightly just before serving.

COOK'S TIP

This salad is good for picnics – to pack it easily, pack the leaves into a large polythene container or unbreakable salad bowl, and nestle the jar of dressing in the centre. Cover with clingfilm. Packed this way, the salad stays crisp and if the dressing leaks during transit, there's no mess.

Grilled Aubergine & Sesame Salad

Serves 4

INGREDIENTS

8 baby aubergines	1 garlic clove, thinly sliced	1 tsp soft light brown sugar
2 tsp chilli oil	1 fresh red bird-eye chilli,	1 tbsp chopped fresh mint
1 tbsp soy sauce	deseeded and sliced	1 tbsp sesame seeds, toasted
1 tbsp Thai fish sauce	1 tsp sesame oil	salt
1 tbsp sunflower oil	1 tbsp lime juice	fresh mint leaves, to garnish

1 Cut the aubergines lengthways into thin slices to within 2.5 cm/1 inch of the stem end. Place in a colander, sprinkling with salt between the slices and set aside to drain for about 30 minutes. Rinse in cold water and pat dry with kitchen paper.

2 Mix the chilli oil, soy sauce and fish sauce together and then brush the mixture over the aubergines. Cook under a preheated hot grill or barbecue over hot coals for 6–8 minutes, turning them over occasionally and brushing with more chilli oil glaze, until golden brown and softened. Arrange them on a serving platter.

3 Heat the sunflower oil in wok or frying pan. Stir-fry the garlic and chilli for 1–2 minutes until just beginning to brown. Remove the pan from the heat and add the sesame oil, lime juice, brown sugar and any remaining chilli oil glaze.

4 Add the chopped mint and spoon the warm dressing over the aubergines.

5 Leave to marinate for about 20 minutes, then sprinkle with toasted sesame seeds. Serve garnished with mint leaves.

Oriental Lettuce Cups

Serves 4

INGREDIENTS

8 Cos lettuce leaves, or similar firm lettuce leaves

2 carrots

2 sticks celery

100 g/3½ oz baby sweetcorn cobs

2 spring onions

100 g/3½ oz beansprouts

2 tbsp chopped roasted peanuts

DRESSING

2 tbsp smooth peanut butter

3 tbsp lime juice

3 tbsp coconut milk

2 tsp Thai fish sauce

1 tsp caster sugar

1 tsp grated fresh root ginger

¼ tsp Thai red curry paste

1 Wash and trim the lettuce leaves, leaving them whole. Arrange on a serving plate or on individual plates.

2 Trim the carrots and celery and cut into fine matchsticks. Trim the sweetcorn and onions and slice both diagonally.

3 Toss together all the prepared vegetables with the beansprouts. Divide the salad mixture evenly between the individual lettuce cups.

4 To make the dressing, place all the ingredients in a screw-top jar and shake well until thoroughly mixed.

5 Spoon the dressing evenly over the salad cups and sprinkle with the chopped peanuts. Serve the salad immediately.

COOK'S TIP

Choose leaves with a deep cup shape to hold the salad neatly. If you prefer, Chinese leaves may be used in place of the Cos lettuce. To remove the leaves from the whole head without tearing them, cut a thick slice from the base end so the leaves are not attached by their stems, then gently ease away the leafy parts.

Thai-style Carrot & Mango Salad

Serves 4

INGREDIENTS

4 carrots
1 small, ripe mango
200 g/7 oz firm tofu
1 tbsp chopped fresh chives

DRESSING
2 tbsp orange juice
1 tbsp lime juice
1 tsp clear honey
1/2 tsp orange-flower water

1 tsp sesame oil
1 tsp sesame seeds, toasted

1 Peel and coarsely grate the carrots. Peel the mango and thinly slice the flesh away from the stone.

2 Drain the tofu, pat dry with kitchen paper and cut into 1 cm/1/2 inch dice. Toss together with the carrots and mango in a salad bowl.

3 For the dressing, place all the ingredients in a screw-top jar and shake well to mix evenly.

4 Pour the dressing over the salad and toss well to coat the salad evenly.

5 Just before serving, toss the salad lightly and sprinkle with chopped chives. Serve immediately.

COOK'S TIP

A food processor will grate the carrots in seconds and is especially useful for time-saving if you're catering for a crowd.

Bamboo Shoot Salad

Serves 4

INGREDIENTS

2 shallots

2 garlic cloves

2 tbsp Thai fish sauce

3 tbsp lime juice

½ tsp dried chilli flakes

1 tsp granulated sugar

1 tbsp round grain rice

2 tsp sesame seeds

350 g/12 oz canned bamboo
    shoots, drained and rinsed

2 spring onions, chopped

fresh mint leaves, to garnish

shredded Chinese leaves or
    lettuce, to serve

1 Place the whole shallots and garlic under a preheated medium-hot grill and grill until charred on the outside and tender inside. Remove the skins and place the flesh in a mortar. Crush to a smooth paste with a pestle.

2 Mix the paste with the fish sauce, lime juice, chilli flakes and sugar.

3 Place the rice and sesame seeds in a heavy-based frying pan over low heat and cook to a rich golden brown, shaking the pan to brown

evenly. Remove from the heat and crush lightly in a mortar with a pestle.

4 Use a sharp knife to shred the bamboo shoots into fine matchsticks. Stir the bamboo shoots into the shallot and garlic dressing, tossing well to coat them evenly. Stir in the toasted rice and sesame seeds, then the spring onions.

5 Pile the salad on to a serving dish and surround with shredded Chinese leaves. Garnish with mint leaves and serve.

Hot & Sour Beef Salad

Serves 4

INGREDIENTS

1 tsp black peppercorns
1 tsp coriander seeds
1 dried red bird-eye chilli
¼ tsp five-spice powder
250 g/9 oz beef fillet
1 tbsp dark soy sauce
6 spring onions
1 carrot

¼ cucumber
8 radishes
1 red onion
¼ head Chinese leaves
2 tbsp groundnut oil
1 garlic clove, crushed
1 tsp finely chopped
    lemon grass

1 tbsp chopped fresh mint
1 tbsp chopped fresh coriander

DRESSING
3 tbsp lime juice
1 tbsp light soy sauce
2 tsp soft light brown sugar
1 tsp sesame oil

1 Crush the peppercorns, coriander seeds and chilli in a mortar with a pestle, then mix with the five-spice powder and sprinkle on a plate. Brush the beef all over with soy sauce, then roll it in the spices to coat evenly.

2 Cut the spring onions into 6 cm/2½ inch lengths and then shred them finely lengthways. Place in iced water and leave until curled. Drain well.

3 Trim the carrot and cut it into very thin diagonal slices. Cut the cucumber in half lengthways and scoop out the seeds, then slice the flesh thinly. Trim the radishes and cut into flower shapes, if you like, or leave whole.

4 Slice the onion thinly, cutting each slice from top to root. Roughly shred the Chinese leaves. Toss all the vegetables together in a large salad bowl.

5 Heat the oil in a heavy-based frying pan and fry the garlic and lemon grass until just turning golden brown. Add the beef and press down with a spatula to ensure it browns evenly. Cook, turning it over once, for 3–4 minutes, depending on the thickness. Remove the pan from the heat.

6 Slice the beef thinly and toss into the salad with the mint and chopped coriander. Mix together the dressing ingredients and stir into the pan, then spoon the mixture over the salad. Serve immediately.

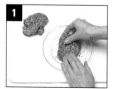

Desserts & Drinks

The normal conclusion to a Thai meal is a basket of fresh, tropical fruits, often including fragrant mangoes, mangosteens, jackfruit, guavas, lychees and rambutans. Thai desserts and sweetmeats are mostly made at home for between-meal treats, or made by experts and reserved for banquets and special occasions, as their preparation can be time-consuming and often requires skillful blending and shaping.

Even the simplest fruits in chilled sugar syrups are delicately scented with jasmine or rose, usually served with little mouthfuls of sticky rice. Others are gently poached in creamy coconut milk and sweetened or caramelized with palm sugar. Bananas make frequent appearances, as they grow everywhere, even in gardens.

As in all Thai dishes, the ubiquitous coconut plays a large part in sweet recipes, as coconut milk or cream in sweet custards, in delectable sweet morsels of paste or delicately scented jellied sweetmeats, or shredded for decoration. Rice, usually of the sticky variety, and tapioca are both essential ingredients in many sweets and cakes, often moulded or subtly coloured, soaked in scented syrups or scented with burning incense.

Many Thai drinks are colourful and exotic in flavour, using the abundance of fruits and coconut milk to their best advantage in long, refreshing drinks, sweetened with palm sugar and often with a generous dash of local whisky or other spirit.

Mangoes in Lemon-grass Syrup

Serves 4

INGREDIENTS

2 large, ripe mangoes

1 lime

1 lemon grass stalk, chopped

3 tbsp caster sugar

1 Halve the mangoes, remove the stones and peel off the skins.

2 Slice the flesh into long, thin slices and gently arrange them in a wide serving dish.

3 Remove a few shreds of the rind from the lime for decoration, then cut the lime in half and squeeze out the juice.

4 Place the lime juice in a small pan with the lemon grass and sugar. Heat gently without boiling until the sugar is completely dissolved.

Remove from the heat and set aside to cool completely.

5 Strain the cooled syrup into a jug and pour evenly over the mango slices.

6 Scatter with the reserved lime rind strips, cover and chill before serving. Serve chilled.

COOK'S TIP

To serve this dessert on a hot day, particularly if it is to stand for a while, place the dish on a bed of crushed ice to keep the fruit and syrup chilled.

Exotic Fruit Salad

Serves 6

INGREDIENTS

1 tsp jasmine tea	125 ml/4 fl oz boiling water	1 starfruit
1 tsp fresh root ginger, grated	2 tbsp caster sugar	2 passion fruit
1 strip lime rind	1 pawpaw	
	1 mango	
	½ small pineapple	

1 Place the tea, ginger and lime rind in a heatproof jug and pour over the boiling water. Leave to infuse for 5 minutes, then strain the liquid into a bowl.

2 Add the sugar to the liquid and stir well to dissolve. Leave the syrup until it is completely cool.

3 Halve, deseed and peel the pawpaw. Halve the mango, remove the stone and peel. Peel and remove the core from the pineapple. Cut the flesh of all 3 fruits into bite-size pieces.

4 Slice the starfruit crossways. Place all the prepared fruits in a wide serving bowl and pour over the cooled syrup. Cover with clingfilm and chill for about 1 hour.

5 Cut the passion-fruit in half, scoop out the flesh and mix with the lime juice. Spoon over the salad and serve.

COOK'S TIP

Starfruit have little flavour when unripe and green, but once ripened and turned yellow they become delicately sweet and fragrant. Usually by this stage, the tips of the ridges have become brown, so you will need to remove these before slicing. The easiest and quickest method of doing this is to run a vegetable peeler along each ridge.

Rose Ice

Serves 4

INGREDIENTS

400 ml/14 fl oz water
2 tbsp coconut cream
4 tbsp sweetened condensed milk
2 tsp rosewater

a few drops pink food
  colouring (optional)
pink rose petals, to decorate

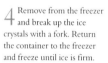

1 Place the water in a small pan and add the coconut cream. Heat the mixture gently without boiling, stirring constantly.

2 Remove from the heat and allow to cool. Stir in the sweetened condensed milk, rosewater and food colouring, if using.

3 Pour into a freezer container and freeze for 1–1½ hours until slushy.

4 Remove from the freezer and break up the ice crystals with a fork. Return the container to the freezer and freeze until ice is firm.

5 Spoon the ice roughly into a pile on a serving dish and scatter with rose petals to serve.

COOK'S TIP

To prevent the ice from thawing too quickly at the table, nestle the base of the serving dish in another dish filled with crushed ice.

Mango & Lime Sorbet

Serves 4

INGREDIENTS

85 g/3 oz caster sugar
100 ml/3½ fl oz water
rind of 3 limes, finely grated
9 tbsp lime juice

2 tbsp coconut cream
2 large, ripe mangoes
curls of fresh coconut, toasted,
   to decorate

1 Place the sugar, water and lime rind in a small pan and heat gently, stirring, until the sugar dissolves. Boil rapidly for 2 minutes to reduce slightly, then remove from the heat and strain into a bowl or jug. Stir in the coconut cream and allow to cool.

2 Halve the mangoes, remove the stones and peel thinly. Chop the flesh roughly and place in a food processor, together with the lime juice. Process to a smooth purée and transfer to a small bowl.

3 Pour the cooled syrup into the mango purée, mixing evenly. Tip into a freezer container and freeze for 1 hour or until slushy in texture. (Alternatively, use an electric ice-cream maker.)

4 Remove the container from the freezer and beat the contents with an electric mixer to break up the ice crystals. Refreeze for a further hour, then remove from the freezer and beat again until smooth.

5 Cover the container, return to the freezer and freeze until firm. To serve, remove from the freezer and leave at room temperature for about 15 minutes before scooping. Scatter with toasted coconut to serve.

COOK'S TIP

If you prefer, canned mangoes in syrup can be used to make the sorbet. Omit the sugar and water and infuse the lime rind in the canned syrup instead.

Lychee & Ginger Sorbet

Serves 4

INGREDIENTS

2 x 400 g/14 oz cans lychees
in syrup
rind of 1 lime, finely grated
2 tbsp lime juice

3 tbsp stem ginger syrup
2 egg whites

TO DECORATE
starfruit slices
slivers of stem ginger

1 Drain the lychees, reserving the syrup. Place the lychees in a blender or food processor with the lime rind, lime juice and stem ginger syrup and process until completely smooth. Transfer to a mixing bowl

2 Mix the purée thoroughly with the reserved syrup, then pour into a freezerproof container and freeze for 1–1½ hours until slushy in texture. (Alternatively, use an ice-cream maker.)

3 Remove from the freezer and whisk to break up the ice crystals. Whisk the egg whites in a clean, dry bowl until stiff, then quickly and lightly fold them into the iced mixture.

4 Return to the freezer and freeze until firm. Serve the sorbet in scoops, with slices of starfruit and ginger to decorate.

COOK'S TIP

It is not recommended that raw egg whites are served to very young children, pregnant women, the elderly or anyone weakened by chronic illness. The egg whites may be left out of this recipe, but you will need to whisk the sorbet a second time after a further hour of freezing to obtain a light texture.

Pineapple with Cardamom & Lime

Serves 4

INGREDIENTS

1 pineapple
2 cardamom pods
1 strip lime rind, thinly pared

1 tbsp soft light brown sugar
3 tbsp lime juice

TO DECORATE
fresh mint sprigs
whipped cream

1 Cut the top and base from the pineapple, cut away the peel and remove the 'eyes' from the flesh. Cut into quarters and remove the core. Slice the pineapple lengthways.

2 Crush the cardamom pods in a mortar with a pestle and place in a small pan with the lime rind and 4 tablespoons of water. Heat until the mixture is boiling, then simmer for 30 seconds.

3 Remove from the heat and add the sugar, then cover and leave to infuse for 5 minutes.

4 Stir in the sugar to dissolve, add the lime juice, then strain the syrup over the pineapple. Chill for 30 minutes.

5 Arrange the pineapple on a serving dish, spoon over the syrup and serve, decorated with mint sprigs and whipped cream.

COOK'S TIP

To remove the 'eyes' from pineapple, cut off the peel, then use a small sharp knife to cut a V-shaped channel down the pineapple, cutting diagonally through the lines of brown 'eyes' in the flesh, to make spiralling cuts around the fruit.

Coconut Custard Squares

Serves 4

INGREDIENTS

1 tsp butter, melted
6 medium eggs
400 ml/14 fl oz coconut milk
175 g/6 oz soft light brown sugar

salt
fruit slices, to serve

TO DECORATE
shreds of coconut
lime rind

1 Brush the butter over the inside of a 19 cm/7½ inch square ovenproof dish or tin, about 4 cm/1½ inch in depth.

2 Beat the eggs together in a large, heatproof bowl and then beat in the coconut milk, brown sugar and a pinch of salt.

3 Place the bowl over a pan of gently simmering water and stir with a wooden spoon for 15 minutes or until it begins to thicken. Pour into the prepared dish or tin.

4 Bake the custard in a preheated oven, 180°C/350°F/Gas Mark 4, for 20–25 minutes until just set. Remove from the oven and allow to cool completely.

5 Turn the custard out of the dish or tin and cut it into squares. Serve decorated with coconut shreds and strips of lime rind together with fruit slices.

COOK'S TIP

Keep an eye on the custard as it bakes, as if it overcooks, the texture will be spoiled. When it comes out of the oven, it should be barely set and still slightly wobbly in the centre, then it will firm up slightly as it cools.

Mung Bean Custards

Serves 6

INGREDIENTS

125 g/4½ oz dried mung beans
2 eggs, beaten
175 ml/6 fl oz coconut milk

100 g/3½ oz caster sugar
1 tbsp ground rice
1 tsp ground cinnamon

TO DECORATE
ground cinnamon
crème fraîche or whipped cream
finely grated lime rind
sliced starfruit
pomegranate seeds

1 Place the beans in a saucepan with enough water to cover. Bring to the boil, then lower the heat and simmer for 30–40 minutes until the beans are very tender. Drain well.

2 Mash the beans, then press through a sieve to make a smooth purée. Place the bean purée, eggs, coconut milk, sugar, rice flour and cinnamon in a large bowl and beat well until mixed.

3 Grease and line the base of 4 x 150 ml/5 fl oz pudding-shaped moulds or ramekin dishes and pour in the mixture. Place on a baking sheet in a preheated oven, 180°C/350°F/Gas Mark 4, and bake for 20–25 minutes or until just set.

4 Cool the custards in the moulds, then run a knife around the edge to loosen and turn out on to serving plates. Sprinkle with cinnamon. Top with a spoonful of crème fraîche or whipped cream and serve with exotic fruit.

COOK'S TIP

To save time use canned mung beans. Omit Step 1, drain the beans thoroughly and continue with Step 2.

Banana Fritters in Coconut Batter

Serves 4

INGREDIENTS

70 g/2½ oz plain flour
2 tbsp rice flour
1 tbsp caster sugar
1 egg, separated
150 ml/5 fl oz coconut milk

4 large bananas
sunflower oil, for deep-frying

TO DECORATE
1 tsp icing sugar
1 tsp ground cinnamon
lime wedges

1 Sift the plain flour, rice flour and sugar into a bowl and make a well in the centre. Add the egg yolk and coconut milk.

2 Beat the mixture until a smooth, thick batter forms. Whisk the egg white in a clean, dry bowl until stiff enough to hold soft peaks. Fold it into the batter lightly and evenly.

3 Heat a 6 cm/2½ inch depth of oil in a large pan to 180°C/ 350°F or until a cube of bread browns in 30 seconds. Cut the bananas in half crossways, then dip them quickly into the batter to coat them.

4 Drop the bananas carefully into the hot oil and fry, in batches, for 2–3 minutes until golden brown, turning once.

5 Drain on kitchen paper. Sprinkle with icing sugar and cinnamon and serve immediately, with lime wedges for squeezing juice as desired.

COOK'S TIP

If you can buy the baby finger bananas that are popular in this dish in the East, leave them whole for coating and frying.

Bananas in Coconut Milk

Serves 4

INGREDIENTS

4 large bananas
350 ml/12 fl oz coconut milk
2 tbsp caster sugar

pinch of salt
½ tsp orange-flower water
1 tbsp shredded fresh mint

2 tbsp mung beans, cooked
fresh mint sprigs, to decorate

1 Peel the bananas and cut them into short chunks. Place in a large pan with the coconut milk, caster sugar and salt.

2 Heat gently until boiling and then simmer for 1 minute. Remove the pan from the heat.

3 Sprinkle the orange-flower water over, stir in the mint and spoon into a serving dish.

4 Place the mung beans in a heavy-based frying pan and place over a high heat until they are turning crisp and golden, shaking the pan occasionally. Remove and crush lightly in a mortar with a pestle.

5 Sprinkle the toasted beans over the bananas and serve warm or cold, decorated with fresh mint sprigs.

COOK'S TIP

If you prefer, the mung beans could be replaced with flaked, toasted almonds or hazelnuts.

Caramel Apple Wedges with Sesame Seeds

Serves 4

INGREDIENTS

115 g/4 oz flour
1 egg
125 ml/4 fl oz water
4 crisp dessert apples

2½ tbsp sesame seeds
250 g/9 oz caster sugar

2 tbsp vegetable oil, plus extra
for deep-frying

1 Place the flour, egg and water in a bowl and whisk well until a smooth, thick batter forms.

2 Core the apples and cut each into 8 wedges. Drop into the batter and stir in the sesame seeds.

3 Put the sugar and 2 tablespoons of oil in a heavy-based pan and heat, stirring, until the sugar dissolves. Continue until the syrup begins to turn golden. Remove from the heat but keep warm.

4 Heat the oil for frying in a wok or deep pan to 180°C/350°F or until a cube of bread turns golden brown in 30 seconds. Lift the apple pieces one by one from the batter, using tongs or chopsticks, and lower into the hot oil and fry for 2–3 minutes until golden brown and crisp.

5 Remove with a perforated spoon and dip very quickly into the sugar mixture. Dip the apple wedges briefly into iced water and drain on non-stick paper. Serve immediately.

COOK'S TIP

Take care not to overheat the sugar syrup or it will become difficult to handle and burn. If it begins to set before you have finished dipping the apple pieces, warm it slightly over the heat until it becomes liquid again.

Thai Rice Pudding

Serves 4

INGREDIENTS

100 g/3½ oz short grain rice
2 tbsp palm sugar
1 cardamom pod, split

300 ml/10 fl oz coconut milk
150 ml/5 fl oz water
3 eggs
200 ml/7 fl oz coconut cream
1½ tbsp caster sugar

sweetened coconut flakes,
    to decorate
fresh fruit, to serve

1 Place the rice and palm sugar in a pan. Crush the seeds from the cardamom pod in a mortar with a pestle and add to the pan. Stir in the coconut milk and water.

2 Bring to the boil, stirring to dissolve the sugar. Lower the heat and simmer, uncovered, stirring occasionally for about 20 minutes until the rice is tender and most of the liquid is absorbed.

3 Spoon the rice into 4 individual ovenproof dishes and spread evenly. Place the dishes in a wide roasting tin with water to come about halfway up the sides.

4 Beat together the eggs, coconut cream and caster sugar and spoon over the rice. Cover with foil and bake in a preheated oven, 180°C/350°F/ Gas Mark 4, for about 45–50 minutes until the custard sets.

5 Serve the rice puddings warm or cold, with fresh fruit and decorated with coconut flakes.

COOK'S TIP

Cardamom is quite a powerful spice, so if you find it too strong it can be left out altogether, or replaced with a little ground cinnamon.

Sticky Rice Balls

Serves 4

INGREDIENTS

300 g/10½ oz glutinous rice
500 g/1 lb 2oz granulated sugar
300 ml/10 fl oz water

pink and green food colourings
rose petals or jasmine flowers,
    to decorate

1 Place the rice in a bowl and add enough cold water to cover. Leave to soak for 3 hours or overnight.

2 Drain the rice and rinse thoroughly in cold water.

3 Line the top part of a steamer with muslin and tip the rice into it. Place the steamer over boiling water, cover and steam the rice for 30 minutes. Remove and set aside to cool.

4 Heat the sugar and water gently until the sugar dissolves. Bring to the boil and boil for 4–5 minutes to reduce to a thin syrup. Remove the pan from the heat.

5 Divide the rice in half and colour one half pale pink, the other half pale green. Shape into small balls.

6 Using 2 forks, dip the rice balls into the syrup.

Drain off the excess syrup and pile on to a dish. Scatter with rose petals or jasmine flowers to decorate.

COOK'S TIP

If you prefer, the rice can be shaped in small sweet moulds or piled into small castle or turret shapes, like dariole moulds.

Banana Pancakes

Serves 6

INGREDIENTS

175 g/6 oz plain flour
pinch of salt
4 eggs, beaten
2 large, ripe bananas, peeled
    and mashed

300 ml/10 fl oz coconut milk
vegetable oil, for frying

TO DECORATE
sliced bananas
6 tbsp lime juice
icing sugar
coconut cream

1 Place the flour, salt, eggs, mashed bananas and coconut milk in a blender or food processor and process until a smooth batter forms. Alternatively, if you don't have a food processor, sift the flour and salt into a bowl and make a well in the centre, then add the remaining ingredients and beat well until smooth.

2 Chill the batter for an hour. Remove from the refrigerator and beat briefly again. Heat a small amount of oil in a small frying pan until very hot.

3 Drop tablespoonfuls of batter into the pan. Cook until the pancakes are golden underneath.

4 Turn over and cook the other side until golden brown. Cook in batches until all the batter is used up, making about 36 pancakes. Remove and drain well on kitchen paper.

5 Serve the pancakes in a stack, decorated with sliced bananas, sprinkled with lime juice and icing sugar and topped with a dollop of coconut cream.

COOK'S TIP

These little pancakes are best eaten hot and freshly cooked, so keep them hot in a low oven while the others are cooking.

Coconut Pancakes

Serves 4

INGREDIENTS

115 g/4 oz flour
3 tbsp caster sugar
pinch of salt
2 eggs
600 ml/1 pint coconut milk

4 tbsp desiccated coconut
vegetable oil, for frying
2 tbsp palm sugar, to decorate
fresh mango or banana, to serve

1 Place the rice flour, sugar and salt in a bowl and add the eggs and coconut milk, whisking until a smooth batter forms. Alternatively, place all the ingredients in a blender and process to a smooth batter. Beat in half the coconut.

2 Heat a small amount of oil in a wide, heavy-based frying pan. Pour in a little batter, swirling the pan to cover the surface thinly and evenly. Cook until pale golden underneath.

3 Turn or toss the pancake and cook quickly to brown lightly on the other side.

4 Turn out the pancakes and keep hot while using the remaining batter to make a total of 8 pancakes.

5 Serve the pancakes folded or loosely rolled, with slices of mango or banana, and sprinkled with palm sugar and the remaining coconut, toasted, if wished.

COOK'S TIP

Rice flour gives the pancakes a light, smooth texture, but if it's not available, you can use ordinary plain flour instead.

Steamed Coconut Cake with Lime & Ginger Syrup

Serves 8

INGREDIENTS

2 large eggs, separated
pinch of salt
100 g/3½ oz caster sugar
5 tbsp butter, melted and cooled
5 tbsp coconut milk
150 g/5½ oz self-raising flour

½ tsp baking powder
3 tbsp desiccated coconut
4 tbsp stem ginger syrup
3 tbsp lime juice

TO DECORATE
3 pieces stem ginger, drained
    and diced
curls of fresh coconut
finely grated lime rind

1 Cut a 28 cm/11 inch round of non-stick paper and press into an 18 cm/7 inch steamer basket to line it.

2 Whisk the egg whites with the salt until stiff. Gradually whisk in the sugar, 1 tablespoon at a time, whisking hard after each addition until the mixture stands in stiff peaks.

3 Whisk in the yolks, then quickly stir in the butter and coconut milk. Sift the flour and baking powder over the mixture, then fold in lightly and evenly with a large metal spoon. Fold in the desiccated coconut.

4 Spoon the mixture into the lined steamer basket and tuck the spare paper over the top. Place the basket over boiling water, cover and steam for 30 minutes.

5 Turn out the cake on to a plate, remove the paper and cool slightly. Mix together the ginger and lime juice and spoon over the cake. Cut into squares and decorate with diced stem ginger, curls of fresh coconut and lime rind.

Strings of Gold

Serves 4

INGREDIENTS

7 egg yolks
1 tbsp egg white
500 g/1 lb 2 oz granulated sugar

200 ml/7 fl oz water
handful of scented
  jasmine flowers

TO SERVE
pomegranate seeds
kiwi fruit, sliced
apple, sliced

1 Press the egg yolks and egg white through a fine sieve, then whisk lightly.

2 Place the sugar and water in a large pan and heat gently until the sugar dissolves. Add the jasmine flowers, bring to the boil and boil rapidly until a thin syrup forms. Remove the flowers with a perforated spoon.

3 Bring the syrup to simmering point. Using a piping bag with a fine nozzle or a paper icing cone, quickly drizzle the egg mixture into the syrup in a thin stream to form loose nests or pyramid shapes.

4 As soon as the threads set, remove the nests carefully and drain well on kitchen paper. Arrange on a warmed serving dish, with the pomegranate seeds, kiwi fruit and apple alongside. Serve at once.

COOK'S TIP

If you can't get hold of fresh, scented jasmine flowers, add a few drops of rosewater or orange-flower water to the syrup instead.

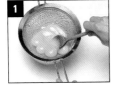

Melon & Ginger Crush

Serves 4

INGREDIENTS

1 melon, about 800 g/1 lb 12 oz
6 tbsp ginger wine
3 tbsp kaffir lime juice
crushed ice
1 lime

1 Peel, deseed and roughly chop the melon. Place it in a blender or food processor with the ginger wine and lime juice.

2 Blend together on high speed until the mixture is completely smooth.

3 Put plenty of crushed ice into 4 tall tumblers. Pour the melon and ginger crush over the ice.

4 Cut the lime into thin slices, cut a slit in each one and slip it on to the side of each glass. Add a slice of lime to each glass as well. Serve immediately.

VARIATION

If you prefer a non-alcoholic version of this drink, simply omit the ginger wine, then top up with ginger ale in the glass. For a change of flavour, use a watermelon when they are in season. Ginger wine is available from specialist wine merchants or liquor stores.

Mango & Coconut Smoothie

Serves 4

INGREDIENTS

2 large, ripe mangoes
1 tbsp icing sugar

500 ml/18 fl oz coconut milk
5 ice cubes, crushed
flaked toasted coconut

1 Cut the mangoes in half and remove the stones. Cut away the peel and coarsely chop the flesh.

2 Place the chopped flesh in a blender goblet or food processor with the icing sugar and blend until completely smooth.

3 Add the coconut milk and ice to the blender or food processor and blend again until frothy.

4 Pour into 4 tall glasses and sprinkle with flaked, toasted coconut to serve.

COOK'S TIP

To add a special kick to the drink (though not perhaps for breakfast!), add a generous dash of white rum to the blender with the coconut milk.

VARIATION

If you don't have shredded, toasted coconut, sprinkle with ground ginger, cinnamon or nutmeg just before serving.

Lime & Lemon Grass Cooler

Serves 4

INGREDIENTS

2 limes
1 small lemon grass stalk
3 tbsp caster sugar
4 ice cubes

125 ml/4 fl oz water
4 lime slices
soda water

TO DECORATE
egg white
caster sugar

1 To decorate the glasses, frost the rims. Pour a little egg white into a saucer. Dip the rim of each glass briefly into egg white and then into caster sugar.

2 Cut each lime into 8 pieces and coarsely chop the lemon grass. Place the lime pieces and lemon grass in a blender or food processor with the sugar and ice cubes.

3 Add the water and process for a few seconds, but not until completely smooth.

4 Strain the mixture into the frosted glasses. Add a lime slice to each glass and top up to taste with soda water. Serve at once.

COOK'S TIP

It's important not to blend the limes for too long – a few seconds is enough to chop them finely and extract the juice. If you process too far, the drink will have a bitter flavour.

Thai Cocktail Sling

Serves 1

INGREDIENTS

2 tbsp whisky
1 tbsp cherry brandy
1 tbsp orange-flavoured liqueur
1 tbsp lime juice

1 tsp palm sugar
dash of Angostura bitters
2 ice cubes

120 ml/4 fl oz pineapple juice
small pineapple wedge,
   to decorate

1 Place the whisky, cherry brandy, liqueur, lime juice, palm sugar and Angostura bitters in a cocktail shaker. Shake well to mix thoroughly.

2 Place the ice cubes in a large glass. Pour the cocktail mixture over the ice, then top up with the pineapple juice.

3 Cut a slit in the pineapple wedge and place on the edge of the glass. Serve immediately.

COOK'S TIP

Scotch whisky is very highly regarded in Thailand, although a powerful whisky is distilled locally – if you have the stomach for it!

COOK'S TIP

If the pineapple juice is quite sweet, as Thai pineapple juice is, you may not need to add sugar. So if you're unsure, taste first.

Tropical Fruit Punch

Serves 6

INGREDIENTS

1 small ripe mango
4 tbsp lime juice
1 tsp finely grated fresh
    root ginger
1 tbsp soft light brown sugar

300 ml/10 fl oz orange juice
300 ml/10 fl oz pineapple juice
100 ml/3½ fl oz rum
crushed ice

TO DECORATE
orange slices
lime slices
pineapple slices
starfruit slices

1 Peel and the mango, remove the stone and chop the flesh. Place in a blender or food processor with the lime juice, ginger and sugar and process until a smooth purée.

2 Add the orange and pineapple juice and the rum and process again for a few seconds until blended.

3 Divide the crushed ice between 6 glasses and pour the punch over the ice. Add orange and lime slices, then decorate the rim of each glass with pineapple and starfruit slices.

COOK'S TIP

To extend the drink a little further and bring out the ginger flavour more, top up each glass with a generous dash of ginger ale.

Index